Dumplings 'N More

OUR STORY

RECOLLECTIONS & RECIPES

Anne Grimes

Dumplings 'N More
Recollections & Recipes

Published by Anne Grimes
Copyright © 2008
Anne Grimes
P.O. Box 98
Ayden, North Carolina 28513

Front cover and food photography
© by Mike Rutherford

Library of Congress Number: 2007933731
ISBN: 978-0-9796418-0-0

Edited and Manufactured
by **Favorite Recipes® Press**
An imprint of

FRP

P.O. Box 305142
Nashville, Tennessee 37230
1-800-358-0560

Art Director: Steve Newman
Book Design: Brad Whitfield and Susan Breining
Project Editor: Tanis Westbrook

Manufactured in the United States of America
First Printing: 2008
20,000 copies

A portion of the proceeds from the sale of *Dumplings 'N More* goes to the Carolina Pregnancy Center.

Dedication

In loving memory of Bryan Grimes, Jr.
March 28, 1939–December 29, 2006

Bryan Grimes, Jr., was a gentle and kind man whose love for his family was only surpassed by the love he had for his Savior and Lord Jesus Christ. Bryan went quietly through life and will be remembered by many for his kindness. Countless others, who never knew him, benefited from his generosity. The world recognizes and applauds a man whose success is measured by his worldly possessions, but his family honors this man for the treasures he built up in heaven, which he now possesses. A man of strength, his courage was shown in the battle he fought for so many years against Lyme disease and the destruction it had on his body. He fought bravely, never complaining, and now he is seated in high places free from the bondage of this disease. A light has gone out here in our lives, but we know that heaven has a bright new star.

Contents

Our Story

6

The Big "Bang" 10   Higher Ground 37
Two Plus Two 13   Life-Changing Events 48
Good Old Days 21   A New Day 53

Harvest Time Recipes 78

Family Favorites 98

Bread for the Journey 136

Food Timeline 170

Awards and Recognition 172

Index 173

Order Information 176

Our Story

Betty Crocker

Home Service Department

1960

Dear Mildred,

May I add my
you must have
the Homemaker of
for your family
of you to say
this award.

Hardly a day passes that my thoughts are not flooded with some wonderful experience that has happened in my life. Needless to say, my life, like everyone else's, has not been a bed of roses, but I have chosen to concentrate on the good things that came my way. For these many years, God has graciously provided for me and my family, and I would unequivocally say, for the most part, "It's been a wonderful life."

Patience is definitely not my long suit, and knowing that, God provided the steady balance I needed in my life for forty-five years in my husband Bryan who, in spite of his illness, was always there for me. Always by our side in the good times and the bad times, God showered us with His mercy and everlasting love. What a joy to get up each morning knowing that no matter what came our way, we were never alone, but always there was that "FRIEND" who would never leave us nor forsake us. Time and time again I have seen His hand at work in our lives and in those around us.

For some time I have known I needed to write these chronicles, these memories, not just for myself lest I forget the details, but for those who need to know that God is no respecter of persons, but that His hand is extended to all who will seek and ask. What marvelous things he can do, not only for me, but also for you. He is the great earth mover; he can move mountains. He can bring joy into our lives when we feel the world is caving in on us. Peace, that wonderful peace, can come in the midst of our most troubled moments. There is no one like Him, and as you walk down memory lane with me, you can see that "He was there all the time" even when we turned in the wrong direction. He looks at our hearts and our desire to do the right thing, and when we fall, He desires to make us strong at our weakest point.

To be blessed with a wonderful, godly, kind husband—whose last fourteen years were surely not only a trial for me, but for him as he bravely fought the destruction that Lyme disease had on his body and mind—a dutiful precious son, a loving daughter-in-law that is really a daughter, and the joy of my life, my granddaughter who calls me on the phone just to say, "Grandma, how are you doing today?" is more than I deserve. Beyond my family, He has blessed me with wonderful friends, a loving church family, loyal employees, faithful customers, and a successful business. With all this naturally comes the material things, and that's just what they are…things, beautiful to look at, but useless in themselves. I liken these things to ornaments we put on the Christmas tree. Without the tree, they are nothing but shiny balls in a box.

Life is not easy. Many reading this have walked the hard road, and you are not alone. Decisions we make oftentimes get us in these hard places, but we all can make a decision to change, to be free from the bondages of sin. It really is a choice. As we walk in the truth of our Lord Jesus Christ, not only will we be changed, but our changed lives will make others want to experience this freedom. I pray that each reader of *Dumplings 'N More* will not only enjoy the reminisces and recipes, but also will find true "soul food" for the partaking.

> *And my soul shall be joyful in the Lord: it shall rejoice in his salvation.*
>
> **Psalms 35:9**

The Big "Bang"

God's divine providence placed me on earth scarcely two months after the famous attack at Pearl Harbor. Although my parents were certainly excited about my arrival, it could hardly have shaken up the world as did this. The newspapers were full of the shocking details of December 7, 1941, and of President Roosevelt's declaring war the next day. The world was in turmoil. What could have been going on in the minds of my parents at that time? With a baby on the way and newly settled in a $3,000 home they had just built on Arlington Drive (now called Arlington Boulevard), in Greenville, North Carolina, surely they had fears of the changes war brings and the disruption to families, and other questions naturally had to be on their minds.

Tension was definitely high in my home at this time as well because by calculation my birth date was supposed to be in December, but I was a ten-month baby, arriving on February 1, 1942. I have always heard that the rich are born with silver spoons in their mouths, but although that was not the case with me, I do believe I was born with a spoon in one hand and a pot in the other, if for no other reason than to make a bang when I came forth—which I most assuredly did. It was common at that time for children to be born at home and such was the situation with me. I was told that at the moment of my birth the bed collapsed. Mother and baby survived, but the bed did not.

My mother was born in Virginia and given the name Mildred Adelaide Taylor, and my daddy wanted to name me after her, but she would have none of that. She absolutely disliked the name Adelaide, but did agree on Mildred. They added Anne which is the name I usually go by.

My daddy, David Clifton Briley, was born in Pitt County, North Carolina, close to Greenville. They were married by a justice of the peace on February 26, 1938. My mother worked as a telephone operator after they were married, but quit before I was born. My daddy started working for a dairy when he was a teenager and later became a milkman, the old timey kind that brought milk to your door in glass bottles with the paper cap on top and the cream line visible through the glass.

Somehow I must have settled right in and enjoyed being the center of attention in our little family. Daddy left each morning to run his milk route and Mother stayed at home keeping us well fed and comfortable. I don't remember anything about my first two years; there are lots of pictures of me all pink, smiley, and healthy, but then my life took a turn just after my second birthday.

I didn't like her! I didn't like her at all. Not only did she take over my crib, but now that I was a "big girl," she had my bottle, that so satisfying warm bottle of milk and corn syrup. Somehow the enemy had moved into my territory, and I had to take back what was mine.

Carefully choosing my weapon, one of my wooden ABC blocks, I hurled it into the crib. Bam! A scream and a flow of blood from the forehead of my baby sister Peggy, born March 24, 1944, alerted me that this was a bad thing. But that scream caused her to release the bottle

> *To make your own*
> **Bedtime Milk Toddy,**
> *combine*
> *8 ounces whole milk,*
> *2 tablespoons corn syrup, and*
> *1/2 teaspoon vanilla*
> *in a microwave-safe glass*
> *or cup. Warm in microwave*
> *and enjoy.*

from her lips, and I grabbed it and dashed under my bed. I could hear footsteps that spelled doom for me. I can almost feel the fear now all these years later.

Had I killed her? No, she was still screaming. The spirit that sent Cain into exile had passed onto me. My parents forgave me, as our Father in Heaven forgives us. You know, they even let me have my bottle back, but it never had that sweet, satisfying fulfillment it once had. Somehow I had become a 'big girl" after all. Sixty-three years later, a small triangular scar on my sister's forehead reminds me of a dastardly deed so long ago and as David in Psalms laments "My sin is ever before me."

Even though the incident of attacking my sister and the memory of the fear of punishment are so real, I can't remember the punishment. I would like to say I have never acted in anger, said bad things, or acted in any other ungodly way since this horrendous incident, but being the human that I am, I can only say I am a sinner, saved by grace.

Looking a little more closely at this incident, it is apparent that at that time my favorite source of food had been cut off and my "addiction" took over. An uncontrollable urge rose up in me and I guess my passion for food began with my corn syrup sweetened milk.

Then they cried unto the Lord in their trouble, and he delivered them out of their distresses.

Psalms 107:6

Two Plus Two

Life was good, and time passed quickly because we were having fun. But then, my grandmother came to visit for a few days and my mother disappeared, reappearing a few days later with a surprise, my baby brother David, Jr., born May 26, 1946. For some reason, jealousy didn't enter the picture this time, and I enjoyed being a big sister and giving him his bottle. He turned out to be the kind of boy who either started or finished anything that was going on, nearly electrocuting himself by sticking a dinner fork into an electric socket when he was three or drinking a whole bottle of Kaopectate at five. His motto was "See it, do it."

The world was a wonder to me, and the yard with its flowers, crepe myrtles, and my daddy's garden gave me a love for the beauty of God's creation. While we actually lived in Greenville, our subdivision, Hillsdale, was more like living in the country. We had a great time watching cows being milked at the dairy farm next door, exploring the cemetery across the road or the smokehouse that Daddy built, or aggravating the chickens we kept. And the clothesline was always so much fun, especially if the wind was blowing and you could run up under the billowing sheets and feel the cool dampness on your face. What an exciting time to grow up with so many interesting things to do outdoors. Simple joys missed by the kids today.

Although we had a wonderful time pursuing such innocent pastimes, it was certainly an exciting day when I finally got to go to school. My parents enrolled me in the local Catholic school for pre-kindergarten, a formidable place with its high ceilings, long hallways, and nuns scurrying around in their black and white habits, all new to me as we went a protestant church. Not only was my

> ## All God's Creatures
>
> *One spring day when I was five, Mother and I were sitting on the porch steps watching a large grasshopper jump from leaf to leaf. Mother remarked that it was the biggest grasshopper she had seen, so it must be very old. Suddenly it jumped out of the bush right into my hair and immediately became entangled in my locks as it tried to get free. Mother tried to disentangle it and said, "I'm going to have to break its legs off to get it out." I began to cry, "No, cut my hair. Don't hurt the grasshopper." She had to cut several strands of my hair to set the grasshopper free. How small a price compared with what Jesus did to set us free. I know how relieved I was to hold that insect in my hand, still intact, and what a joy it was to set it free to jump from leaf to leaf.*

intellect stimulated with a desire to learn, but my palate had some new experiences likewise. For the first time I had sauerkraut on a hotdog and had a tomato dish made from tomatoes that didn't come out of Daddy's garden, canned tomato soup.

It also was during this time that my daddy was given an opportunity to go to Washington, North Carolina, to manage a branch of Carolina Dairies. He had to be there at 2 a.m. to get his route men loaded and ready to run their routes. Then he would return home, have breakfast with us, work in his garden, rest a little, and go back in the afternoon to check his route men back in. One Saturday afternoon, I went back to work with him. There was a dairy bar there, and I was sitting on his desk looking out through a glass at the customers probably thinking how much I would like some ice cream myself.

Somewhere out there was my future husband, an eight-year-old boy, who, looking back through that glass, saw me and said to himself, 'I'm going to marry that girl." This is what he told me years later after I did in fact marry this boy. I would have thought he was joking had he not been able to describe how I was wearing my hair and the dress I had on. I remembered the dress myself because my daddy bought it for me at a dress shop a few doors down from the dairy. How many husbands can remember what you wore today much less years ago? This was a divine appointment, just one of many that God set up in our lives.

Beyond Dick and Jane

During the fall of 1947, while I was in regular kindergarten at the Catholic School, I became ill and that scared me. Dr. Haar put me to bed, and I was not allowed to get up. It seemed like an endless trek of daily visits to his office, with my daddy having to carry me there and back, bottomless glasses of an awful brown iron tonic that could only be drunk through a glass quill so as not to stain my teeth, and needle after needle seeking my last drop of blood. What else could I think? I surely was going to die. As months passed, I didn't seem to be getting better. I spent my days and nights in the bed. Unable to read, I could only look at the pictures in magazines.

Little did I know that I was not the only one with problems. Mother was expecting, and there were some complications. On November 17, 1948, my baby sister Rebecca (Becky) was born. My mother recovered from her problems, but I was still sick.

One day as I complained about being bored, Mother brought me a gold covered book to look at, and it was fascinating. The pictures showed how to mix a cake, bake a cake, and spread icing on a cake. It all looked wonderful, but I wanted to know what the words said, so I began to ask my mother what different words were. Soon I could read complete sentences and all the words. It didn't take Dick and Jane to help me learn to read, but a mother with patience and the 1942 Betty Crocker Cookbook.

At the time I was sick, I didn't know that I had rheumatic fever and a heart murmur and that bed rest along with the tonics and blood work were the prescriptions for getting well. Little by little my strength returned and the aching in my legs left. All the time I lay in bed reading the Betty Crocker cookbook, I was envisioning getting into Mother's kitchen and cooking some of that fabulous looking food pictured in the book. I would ask Mother to cook some of the recipes, especially the 1-2-3-4 cake layer recipe. She kept telling me it was not a real Betty Crocker recipe but one that my grandmother had used for years. Boy, when Mother put her fresh coconut filling between the layers and the Seven Minute Icing on top, it was like heaven in my mouth.

In the center of that 1942 cookbook were two pages in color showing gastronomical delights only enhanced by my imagination, and right in the middle was a Swedish tea ring. My mouth watered as I pondered over the centerfold, and then I would turn a few pages over to look at the pictures on how to make bread. Even today, breads are my favorite foods.

The day finally came when I was allowed up, and off to the kitchen I went. My first endeavor in my cooking career was hot chocolate—still working on the warm milk "addiction." I don't exactly remember the recipe, but I'm sure it was good to me.

I needed an apron that said "Cook in Progress." I just love aprons and if you see me in the kitchen, you will see an apron. Sometimes I forget to take it off and you will see me working in the yard (my other passion) with my apron on.

While most girls were thinking about dolls and such, I was interested in kitchen gadgets. If you opened my kitchen drawers today, you would think I owned Williams Sonoma. My kitchen cabinets are overflowing with gadgets and pans of all shapes and sizes for almost any cooking project. And you'd better believe it, that 1942 Betty Crocker cookbook was not my last. I have a wall of cookbooks, many more than one hundred years old, which are so interesting to me. The study of food history has accompanied my interest in cooking. However, I have to say that my interest in food, beginning at a very early age, was sealed during this illness, another of the wonderful ways in which the Lord has worked in my life.

My Grandmothers

During my growing up years, both my grandmothers would pay us visits, and since both were excellent cooks we enjoyed the fruits of their culinary skills. Both were also seamstresses and made beautiful clothes.

My grandmother Taylor, born Mary Rebecca Sermons but called Mamie, lived in the back apartment in a house on Evans Street in Greenville. My granddaddy Taylor, Charles Kinchin Taylor, died when I was small. I can still smell the tea cakes my grandmother baked. She would not let us have any of the freshly baked cookies because she said they needed to be mellowed and would store them in a coffee can. She kept a backup can of those buttery delights, and we'd sit on her back porch smelling the four o'clocks and eating those cookies with a big glass of milk, thinking it couldn't get any better than this. Another one of my favorites that she made was Peach Pandowdy, a kind of cobbler-pie.

Grandmother Taylor took in sewing, and I've heard that if you showed her a dress, she could take your measurements and make a pattern out of the newspaper. She had a good voice, and I remember her sitting on our front porch in the

Grandma Taylor's
Old-Fashioned Tea Cakes
Cream 1 cup sugar and
1 cup (2 sticks) butter in a mixing
bowl until light and fluffy.
Add 2 eggs, one at a time,
beating well after each addition.
Add 1 tablespoon water and
1 teaspoon vanilla extract and mix well.
Sift together 4 cups all-purpose flour,
1 teaspoon baking powder and a dash of salt.
Add to the creamed mixture and mix well.
Cover and chill for 1 hour.
Preheat the oven to 350 degrees.
Roll out the chilled dough to a thickness
slightly less than 1/4-inch. Cut into rounds
using a 2-inch biscuit cutter or a glass.
Arrange on an ungreased baking sheet and
bake for 12 to 15 minutes or until
lightly browned. This recipe makes
about 6 dozen.

evening singing the song that Kate Smith made popular, "When the Moon Comes Over the Mountain." I can see her now, rocking and singing away. A source of amazement to me was her long hair, which she plaited into two braids that she wound around her head and pinned into place. She had three daughters Lila, Grace, and the middle daughter Mildred, my mother. She lost an infant son.

I would go visit my Grandmother Briley, born Jennie Lynn Whitehurst, a lot during the summer months, and we became a traveling duo. I learned to love gardening and canning from watching her efforts. It seemed like she would stay up all night putting up tomatoes and succotash (corn, butterbeans, and tomatoes). I never remember going to her house that she didn't have food on her stove top. I could always find a piece of fried chicken and fried corn bread patties.

She didn't drive, so when she wanted to visit her daughters we rode the bus. We would go visit Ethel, Marylene, or Susie, and I have fond memories of the times with them. She had six daughters and one son, my daddy. She lost an infant daughter Mildred. Jennie and Virginia lived close by, and Elsie lived at home, as she was a teenager when I was born. Grandmother Briley sewed too, and I remember some jumpers that she made for me for school that I absolutely loved. My grandmother and granddaddy, Fenner Briley, were separated. He had been a farmer, but lost his farm during the depression, and later was a carpenter. He lived with us a while during the time he was converting our attic into two more bedrooms and a bath. We needed it because there were six of us sharing two bedrooms.

A poem I wrote when I was twenty-six called "Grandma" was published in a local paper

Grandma

I watch her from the doorway,
Wondering, if she's thinking of tomorrow or
yesterday.
Of the beans she's picking,
If they'll be as good as last year's.
Or of Mama's corn relish.
Whatever happened to her recipe?
Of hot days when she was just a girl.
Giggling over the boys from down the road.
Of meeting him,
Boy, were they young,
Marriage and all the family things.
Or of children all now grown,
Some near, some far away.
Of Susie's child coming next week
Oatmeal cookies, or chocolate cake?
Or who will plow next year's garden,
Old Doc has passed away
And how can sister keep going?
Her rheumatism gets worse.
Of summer days hence
When the weeds have taken over,
And all she can do is watch.
And of days when she'll be sipping honey
Instead of picking beans.

and depicted my reflections on this godly woman whose love for her garden passed on to me. Gardening and being outdoors fall just behind my love for cooking. For years I have had a greenhouse, and today as I am writing this it is 42 degrees outside, but I am looking at a big bowl of strawberries from my greenhouse.

Family time was the norm back then and grandparents didn't live so far away. We used to sing that song; "Over the river and through the woods to Grandmother's house we'll go." And it wasn't just a song; it was a real event. We felt safe and secure in our families and in our little neighborhood, hardly realizing what was going on in the world beyond our doorstep.

> *Thou wilt show me the path of life:*
> *in thy presence is fulness of joy; at thy right hand*
> *there are pleasures for evermore.*
>
> **Psalms 16:11**

The Smell of Clover

Although I loved school, summers were a special time. While my daddy was an avid fisherman, he didn't like getting in the water and never learned to swim, and my mother almost drowned once. so our getting them to take us to the beach was almost impossible. We worried them so much one summer that my daddy decided to take care of it once and for all. A big truck drove up one day and dumped a load of sand in our backyard. From out of nowhere, a yard man showed up and began to rake it out in a big circular shape. Then my daddy came home and began to assemble a hose with a funny twirling thing on it. Afterwards, he began to unload poles and a big green canvas from his truck.

By the next day, there it was in all its glory, something nobody else in the neighborhood had, and as it was presented to us by my daddy, "Now you have your own beach, Briley's beach."

And so we did. We had a nice sandy area with water sprinklers to cool us off. We had our own bathhouse in the form of a large green army tent. We had our own concession stand in the washhouse, a refrigerator with a freezer that had all kinds of popsicles, ice cream sandwiches, pushups, and to drink, little bottles of chocolate milk. We had more friends than you could feed, and my parents had to run some of them home because they wanted to camp out in the tent. With our own beach and free treats, we were the envy of the neighborhood. What parents we had!

On rainy, cold days when we couldn't play outside, we could go to the movies. The price of a movie was 7 cents, then later rose to 11 cents. On Saturday mornings there were special shows, and we could use RC Cola caps to get in to the movie. Oftentimes there would be a live show before the cartoon started. I especially liked the magic shows and the animals that performed tricks. After the movie we sometimes ran down to White's Department store where we could smell the onions they used for topping their hot dogs before we even got in the door.

We never lacked for things to do, and you never heard us say we were bored. Daddy always had inventive things for us to do, called work. He, like me, was into gadgets and bought Mother an ironing press, like an electric ironing board with a set of rollers, and we all learned to iron sheets and pillowcases, even my brother. Daddy had a garden tractor that you could stand on and ride, so he assembled a set of lawn mower

Mother's Lettuce Slaw
Combine 1/2 cup Miracle Whip Salad Dressing,
3 tablespoons vinegar,
2 tablespoons sugar and 1/2 teaspoon celery seeds in a bowl and mix well.
Let it stand until the sugar dissolves. Combine 1 head lettuce, cut in half and thinly sliced, 1/4 cup finely chopped green bell pepper, and 1/4 cup finely chopped onion in a large bowl. Drizzle with the dressing just before serving and toss gently. This will serve 6 to 8.

blades behind it, and we had the first riding lawnmower in the neighborhood. We all had big yards, and it wasn't long before we were mowing lawns for 50 cents a pop. We were the Briley Lawn Mower Service. Quite an entrepreneurial bunch we were. Many a time we were trying to beat the summer rainstorms, with the winds blowing and the thunder off in the distance, to get that half dollar.

One of my fondest memories is the smell of frying fish wafting from my mother's kitchen on Friday evenings, the time we cut our own yard. When we finished, we knew that we'd have a big platter of crisp butterfish, her lettuce slaw, and a big mound of crunchy corn bread patties alongside a pitcher of iced tea waiting for us. What a treat on a hot summer evening after sweating for what seemed like hours getting our lawn ready for the weekend.

The lawn, too, had its own aroma. We didn't have centipede grass or zoysia back then, but huge swaths of clover that smelled so good when newly cut. The swaths were teeming with honeybees all out to get nectar for the Sioux Bee Clover Honey we kept in the kitchen cabinet for our biscuits. We had to step quickly through the clover with our bare feet lest those bees take offense at our stomping their turf.

You could hear the squeals from our backyard on Sunday afternoons as we dropped ice down one another's back and then ran away. What's a hot summer afternoon without homemade ice cream? It was a treat for the four of us to be

hauled into town to the ice house on Albemarle Avenue to get a 50 cent big bag of crushed ice. We watched excitedly as they dragged a big rectangular block of ice with big ice tongs from the icy inner sanctum behind wooden doors. Then the block of ice the size we needed was chipped off to go into the ice crusher. The grinding noise was such beautiful music to our ears because we knew we'd soon be on our way back home where Mother had a big pot of ice cream custard made up ready to go in the hand-cranked cedar White Mountain freezer. Those old cedar ice cream freezers are getting top dollar on eBay right now, and I've been tempted!

We took turns cranking the freezer, and it seemed like forever before one of us would holler, "It's ready!" We'd eat until we had headaches; it seems homemade ice cream is colder than that from the home refrigerator freezer. We had those brightly colored aluminum tumblers that are coming back into style now (they're on eBay too), and they would get so cold and frosty on the outside the napkin would freeze to the sides. After we had our fill, Mother would make one more batch to put in our freezer for later. We mostly had chocolate because that was Daddy's favorite and even though he worked for a dairy, I know he thought homemade was the best.

Making homemade ice cream at my house today is still a special time. Though the ice houses are all gone and my ice cream freezer doesn't even use ice, I still have memories of those days. I keep homemade ice cream in my freezer all the time and, until Daddy died in 1999, he would come by my house and help himself, and I always made sure there was chocolate there for him. I always knew if he had been by while we were at work because he would leave a spoon in the sink.

Holidays to Remember

Summer was not summer without a garden, and from the time I was small I remember an old black man who came each year to help Daddy prepare the garden. He always looked dirty and unkempt, and I had a hard time understanding him because he stuttered. He was called Brother Doc. I didn't know where he lived, but he always knew when to show up to work in the yard and garden. He would walk behind his push plow and sing Negro spirituals and we kids would sit on the steps just to hear those mournful sounds. But it is not those times I remember most.

Each year Brother Doc would come by around Thanksgiving to get a little gift for the holidays and I would see Daddy give him some money and fruit, canned goods, or whatever we had. The year I was eight, he showed up on a cold Thanksgiving Day. Mother was just getting

"Old Tom" out of the oven and there he was at the door, blowing smoke and rubbing his hands. Mother invited him in and said Daddy would be back in a few minutes. He said, "It sure smells good." Mother turned to him and said, "Are you hungry?" "Yes'm," he replied. She told him to come to the dining room with her. Dining room? We never got to use the dining room; it was for guests. She sat him down at the table and went back and started slicing turkey.

She didn't fix him a plate, she fixed him a platter. Then she took the cover off the coconut cake, its smell permeating the air as she cut him a hunk of it, and put it on the dining room table. Something was going on here. How could this dirty shabby man be eating at our dining room table? I heard a sob and peeped through the doorway. Tears were running down his face. I heard him begin to pray in his stuttering voice. He went on and on giving thanks. How could

he have so much to be thankful for? His food was getting cold. Somehow I knew Mother had done something extraordinary that day.

Daddy came in and sat at the table talking to him while he ate. He sent him on his way with a gift and a parting, "See you in the spring." Spring came, but Brother Doc didn't come back. It turned out he was homeless and got sick and died that winter. This memory has stayed with me all these years, and I have come to realize that this is how God looks at us, past all the dirt and grime, past all the imperfections, and with his heart of love and compassion seats us at His table and prepares a feast for us. Are we, who have so much, grateful for all that He provides and humbly before Him pour out our thanks? This was one Thanksgiving that I will never forget.

Greenville always had a Christmas Parade that went downtown from Dickinson to Five Points and then turned and went down Evans toward the river. It was usually held on a school afternoon the week before we got out of school for Christmas, and we would walk from the school to downtown to watch it. It was always so exciting to hear the band playing before we could see it. There was always a radio broadcast of the parade and an interview with Santa Claus for those who couldn't make it downtown to the see the parade in person.

Another exciting pre-holiday radio program featured the reading of letters to Santa Claus. The announcer called Santa in the North Pole and read him the letters we had sent to the radio station. We were glued to the radio, listening for him to read our letter to Santa and, of course, Santa always said we had been good and he wouldn't miss our house on his trip to Greenville on Christmas Eve. How exciting!

Christmas without special foods would be like Santa without his beard; it just wouldn't seem right. I can remember sitting at the table with Mother, peeling off the orange rinds while she was laboring away at grating the fresh coconut, some to go in the ambrosia and some for the coconut cake you will keep hearing about. Daddy always brought home lots of extra cream at Christmas because on Christmas Eve Mother would make a big bowl of homemade eggnog, that rich creamy goodness flavored with vanilla for us kids, and a shot of bourbon added for the grown-ups. We all had that "got milk" mustache because it was mighty good stuff.

Our countertop was laden with walnuts, pecans, and Brazil nuts, and Daddy's favorites, the chocolate drops with the white creamy filling and the peanut squares. We all had our hands in the big box of chocolate-covered peanuts made then, as they are now, by the Old Dominion

Company in Virginia. Something that I seldom see now but was always on the counter, a box of Muscat raisins, seeded grapes dried on the stems. But the biggest treat for us all was to be allowed in the living room to see the fragrant cedar tree all adorned and lit up. Right on the coffee table was Mother's cut glass candy dish full of her homemade fudge, chock full of pecans. Our hands sometimes weren't quick enough, and we'd be admonished, "How about leaving some for somebody else!" How much more could you ask for?

We always found one more thing we thought we needed for Christmas, but while we didn't get everything we asked for, we certainly didn't lack. After all, Santa resided in our living room, that is a great big, six-foot-tall cardboard replica of Santa drinking a Coca-Cola that some store owner had given Daddy once after Christmas was over.

Fudge didn't last long at our house when I was growing up. There were four sets of hands not only waiting to grab the spoon to scrape the pot, but also to get the first piece of warm fudge. Naturally, Mother had to make more than one batch if Daddy was to have any when he got home!

To make
Mother's Chocolate Fudge*,*
combine 2 cups sugar,
2/3 cup evaporated milk,
1/4 cup (1/2 stick) butter,
2 tablespoons dark corn syrup, and
2 ounces unsweetened chocolate in a heavy saucepan. Bring to a rolling boil, stirring constantly. Boil for exactly 3 minutes. Remove from the heat and let stand for 10 minutes. Beat with a wooden spoon until thickened. Stir in 1 teaspoon vanilla extract and 1 cup chopped pecans. Pour quickly into an 8×8-inch buttered pan. Let stand until firm. Cut into squares.

A Christmas Lesson

During my high school years, like it is today, fashion was a big topic. We had gone through the poodle coat phase and were into the suede coat phase. When I was in the tenth grade, my friends were sporting the new suede coats in different colors, and I had my heart set on a blue one. I told my parents that this was all I wanted for Christmas, but Mother told me they were very expensive. Christmas came, and I got a suede coat, but it wasn't blue. I was very upset. Daddy said that the coat only came in dark brown and tan, and they got me a tan one. I threw the coat down and went out of the room. When I returned, Mother said to hang it up and they would take it back. The chair I had thrown the coat on had a newspaper in it. When I picked up the coat, right on the back was the imprint of the day's news. Mother said we couldn't take coat back now because it was messed up and that I was going to have to pay to have it cleaned. It cost me $15 to have the coat cleaned.

I finally wore it to school about two weeks later. When my friends saw my coat, they went wild and kept telling me how lucky I was. I was confused; what was so special about this coat? I told them I really wanted a blue coat, and one of my friends said, "But you have the real thing." How was it different from theirs? They had something called heek suede and I had real suede. I was stunned. Their families were much better off financially than mine, yet my parents bought me a real suede coat.

I later found out that the coat cost $125. That was a lot of money in 1958. Mother did not get a gift that Christmas so I could have my coat. I was so ashamed and wondered if they regretted giving me what I asked for. I know I must have hurt them terribly for being so ungrateful. I think about the times we are so ungrateful to God for the things God brings into our lives and how he must be offended that we care so little about his generosity. They forgave me and loved me still. I thank God every day for parents who set such examples before me.

The scripture that comes to mind here is Matthew 7:9-11. "Or what man is there of you, whom if his son ask bread, will he give him a stone? Or if he ask a fish, will he give him a serpent. If ye then, being evil, know how to give good gifts unto your children, how much more shall your Father which is in Heaven give good things to them that ask Him?"

A Chance to Shine

In 1950, a new cookbook showed up at our house, the Betty Crocker Picture Cookbook. If I thought the 1942 edition was something, this new cookbook blew my socks off. It was like a Sears Roebuck catalog—you wanted one of everything.

I had logged in quite a few hours in the kitchen by the time I was nine, and while I'm sure Mother wanted the kitchen to herself at times, she had such patience. Mother was an experimenter in the kitchen and changed recipes according to what she had available. She made up names for dishes she created. We had French this, Italian that, German this, Swedish that. She discovered mushrooms as an ingredient one day and we began to have mushrooms in all kinds of dishes. Daddy never did like mushrooms, and he would pick them out and put them in a bowl. B.G., our son, does the same thing.

Mother always said a dish needed not only to taste good, but be pleasing to look at, and a table needed to look good and be set right. After looking at the beautiful pictures in the cookbook, I knew that how food looked was important. Those pictures sure sold me.

I really loved baking, and one day I got my chance to shine. A death in the neighborhood meant we needed to provide a cake, and Mother did not have time to bake one. There wasn't a deli-bakery on every corner like there is now, so I got to bake a cake, a funeral cake. Evidently it was a hit because Mother received a lot of compliments, but she proudly told them I had baked it.

Next a neighbor needed a birthday cake, and while I had not learned to decorate cakes back then, I could make a pretty cake, so I sold my first cake. A light went off in my head, so after discussing my idea with my parents, they decided I could go out and solicit some cake business. I think they thought it wouldn't amount to much—my being just nine years old—but soon I was baking four to six cakes every Saturday for neighbors.

As word spread, I began to get orders from outside our neighborhood, and at times Mother had to help me. After all, those 1-2-3-4 butter cakes can't be beat—and we did have butter. I charged $3 for a three-layer, nine-inch cake and offered five varieties: devil's food with Seven Minute Icing, and yellow cake with chocolate, coconut, pineapple, or orange-lemon icing. I learned to milk a coconut, crack it, peel it, and grate it for the delicious coconut filling Mother taught me to make. I wouldn't take less than $30 for that cake today. Mother would deliver the cakes for me outside our neighborhood, and I would hand deliver the rest. I got to keep half the money.

One of my customers would call repeatedly inquiring when her cake would be ready because she wanted it delivered while it was still warm. I would hurry over to her house as soon as the Seven Minute Icing got on the devil's food layers. When I quit baking cakes on a regular basis, she still wanted one when I had time. Loyal customers are a blessing!

Growing Up

During the pre-puberty years, girlfriends took on a new meaning. After all, you can't tell your mother everything—at least that's what we thought. While our neighborhood was full of kids, there were only two girls my age, Alice and Mary Alice. We shared secrets, rode the bus together to school, had slumber parties, and all the usual things girls do when they are eleven and twelve.

Then at school I had a special friend, Susan, who moved into our school district in the sixth

Keeping Up Appearances

Mother always said there was a right and wrong way to do anything and appearances meant a great deal. She said people judge you by what they see, so don't do anything that looks bad, don't say anything that sounds bad, and don't do rummage sales; it looks bad for your family.

Mary Alice invited me to spend the weekend with her. She was the youngest of six so she had older siblings that had taught her more of the ways of the world than I could ever have imagined. That weekend, it seems that her two older sisters were going to have a rummage sale downtown on Dr. Brown's front lawn next to the fruit stand (his sister who taught music charged a small amount for a space) and two doors down from White's Department Store. We were going with them to help spread the clothes out on the hedges out front.

As it turned out, the two older sisters saw some b-o-y-s of interest and we were left to sell the clothes and collect the money. Somehow Mother had reason to be coming down Dickinson Avenue, and there was her daughter peddling clothes off bushes, no matter that it was a doctor's front yard. I thought we were doing a great job.

I had collected about $1.50 and we had just a few pieces left when suddenly, my ear was almost jerked off my head. Mother had parked and came up behind me and was towing me off. "No daughter of hers was going to peddle in the streets." I'm surprised I was ever able to hear properly out of that ear again after she used it to pull me to the car. That would be child abuse today.

I still had that $1.50 in my pocket, and Mary Alice said I could keep it; my throbbing ear said I had earned it. Some months later, Mother had a birthday and I used that money to buy her a beautiful glass vase from Belks. She made a big to-do over how pretty it was and set it on the fern stand in the living room. She never asked me how I was able to afford such a nice vase, and I didn't tell. When she died, I found a small sticker on the bottom of the vase that said Rummage Sale—Anne. Mothers know more than they let on. It now sits on that same fern stand in my house.

grade. One day, she invited me home to lunch. If you lived close enough to school you could go home for lunch, and Susan lived about three blocks away with her aunt and uncle. I'm sure they weren't expecting company for lunch.

There were three of them and three pork chops. Her Aunt Bebe was so gracious in welcoming me into their home and never missed a beat. This special lady has remained in my memories as the hostess I would like to be. She never knew the impact that lunch had on me. Now, how often do we thank those who have imparted special gifts into our lives?

Susan, an avid horsewoman, all these years later has come back into my life in a very special way as a sounding board and a powerful prayer warrior. God knows when we're going to need the strengths others have, and here again I believe he set up a divine appointment several years ago when she reentered my life by coming to our business to pick up some of our Anne's Chicken Base. We had not seen each other since high school, but I feel there was a bond that had never broken all those years. God is so good!

Our neighborhood was growing, and new restaurants were springing up. The West End Circle Drive-In was a popular place to go to eat. Hot dogs were 10 cents, and Daddy could get a dozen hot dogs for a dollar, a six-pack of cokes for 25 cents plus deposit, and we had a meal fit for a king. Across the Tar River on the other side of town was Respass Barbeque, known for its Brunswick stew and corn sticks as well as barbeque. And right down the street from us lived the Hardees. Wilbur Hardee was in the restaurant business and had opened the Silo restaurant on Highway 11 right at the end of our subdivision. We were allowed to ride our bikes down there and go to the window and buy french fries. He had a big sign that had a chicken with a bag of golf clubs that said "Chicken in the Rough," meaning he had fried chicken. In 1960, Mr. Hardee opened the first Hardees Drive In located in Greenville. Later, he sold the Hardees name and business to Jim Gardner from Rocky Mount. Just down the road on Highway 11 was the South 11 Drive-In movie, a very popular place because a carload could get in for one price. As the years passed, it became more popular to eat out and new restaurants sprang up all over town, especially in the downtown area where East Carolina College was located.

Another event in 1954 caused the world to take notice, especially here in our state of North Carolina. Hurricane Hazel came through, causing unbelievable damage with twenty-five thousand homes destroyed and twenty lives lost. This was the most destructive hurricane to ever hit North Carolina. We were aware of a storm's coming, but because there were so few televisions and we did not yet own one, we did not have up-to-date weather information.

Our school superintendent sent the buses out to pick us up in the morning as usual on October 15, but by lunchtime my daddy had unloaded his milk truck and was at the school picking up the neighborhood kids. It was already raining, and the wind was blowing.

Mother herded us all into the living room—a special treat for us because usually it was only at Christmas that all the doors were opened to the living room and dining room. Daddy packed a cooler with small Cokes and chocolate milk in case we got we got thirsty in the night. Mother had a picnic basket in the middle of the floor full of fried chicken, loaf bread, and Lance cheese crackers. That square meal was our standby for any occasion. Daddy had a box with several flashlights and an Aladdin kerosene lantern as well as two big jugs of water. A pile of blankets and sheets and pillows were on the sofa. We had the radio on, but then it went out when the lights went off.

Silence reigned as we tried to make out each other in the dark while Daddy fumbled with lighting the lantern. That night was a frightening one for us all as we lay cowered on the floor in our darkened living room, the window cracked so that the panes would not blow out from the pressure, and listened as we heard our pecan trees fall. What a horrendous sight at daybreak! Our beautiful yard was a disaster, but God had protected us as not one tree hit our home and we were all safe. Across from the pasture we could see the silo at the dairy farm on its side. My brother couldn't wait to get over there to check it out. We were so thankful for the mercy of God in our neighborhood, so much physical damage, but all lives were intact.

Sadly, later on that fall, Daddy had a heart attack at age thirty-nine. It was a blow to the structure of our family life as he was not able to work. His boss, John Webb, put him on a leave of absence with pay, but it is heartbreaking to see your daddy debilitated and not able to do anything except stay in bed. We all stood there watching him cry when he heard that he would not be able to work for a long time, and then I remembered my own ordeal and wondered if he had the same fears I did. Healing took place as God restored his body, and years later he was told it didn't look like he had ever had a heart attack. He lived to be eighty-four and was driving the day before he died in 1999.

It is God that girdeth me with strength and maketh my way perfect.
Psalms 18:32

Here we were, lost as a goose. It was a big transition from our little school where we knew everybody and most of the kids were from our neighborhood. Suddenly we were thrown together with two other classes of eighth graders and a lot of upperclassmen who were "grown." The girls were wearing lipstick and had crinolines under their skirts.

The old Greenville High School was situated beside a big ravine and across the street from the city swimming pool. The school was overcrowded and we were waiting for the completion of the new Rose High School on Elm Street. But in the meantime, some of us were having classes in the coal room. The biggest topic of interest that year was Little Rock, Arkansas, and integration. We were introduced that year to algebra, French, and high school boys. Suddenly the boys our age

were silly, but these older guys had class. New friends were made, and we had loads of fun at Carole's house, where her mother baked the first blonde brownies I had ever had. Boy, were they good! You bet I got the recipe.

Beginning the Rest of My Life

The summer I was 15, I was back helping my daddy at the dairy bar, riding back and forth with him every day. When they moved the dairy to River Road, he had a route supervisor who went in early to get the route men going, so Daddy worked more regular hours. Halfway through the summer, a young man started coming in with his pig-tailed sister, usually to get a milkshake if he had the money and just to talk if he didn't. He never really introduced himself, and I never got into much serious conversation with him. I had a job to do, and he seemed like he was a lot older since he was going off to college in the fall.

When summer ended, I quit working except on weekends. One of the ladies in the office, Miss Rosalie, said the young man had left me a note asking me to write him. When I looked at that pink piece of paper, I saw the name Bryan Grimes and thought it was a joke.

I rode through Grimesland every time I came to Washington, and Bryan Grimes was a major general in the Civil War who had been dead for years, so I didn't respond.

Carole's Blonde Brownies
Preheat the oven to 350 degrees. Cream 1½ cups granulated sugar, 1½ cups packed brown sugar, and 3/4 cup (1½ sticks) softened butter in a mixing bowl until fluffy. Beat in 2 eggs and 2 teaspoons vanilla extract. Stir in 2 cups self-rising flour, 2 cups (12 ounces) chocolate chips, and 1½ cups chopped pecans. Spoon into a greased and floured 9×13-inch baking pan. Bake 20 to 25 minutes or until a wooden pick inserted in the center comes out clean. Do not over-bake. Makes about 24 brownies.

I found out from Miss Rosalie, who knew his family, that Bryan Grimes was his real name. One Saturday he showed up home from college, and feeling a little sorry for him, I told him that the next time he was home, he should come to supper. He made it back to school and called me about supper, so I set a date. Having learned the importance of how food looked as well as tasted and how important it was to be gracious, I guess I just decided to "put on the dog" for him. I talked Mother into letting me use the dining room, which was only for special occasions, and went to the grocery store to pick out my meal.

He had to be impressed, although, at the time, I think I did this more for me than for him because he really hadn't made the bells ring for me. I served ham steak with grilled pineapple rings, butterbeans, mashed potatoes, sliced tomato and lettuce, rolls, and chocolate cake, all washed down with our Southern sweet tea. In two weeks he made it back to my doorstep asking me to go off with him. Mother let me, which was a surprise to me since he was three years older, but she liked him.

If a first date could be a fiasco, this was it. We were to pick up his cousin Alice in Robersonville and take her to his grandmother's in Washington, go to the Rendezvous, a family restaurant, to eat, and then to Camp Leach, an Episcopal camp where Bryan had been a lifeguard, to meet with other counselors and lifeguards from the previous summer. We picked up his cousin in his grandmother's car, but that was the end of the plans.

Just outside Washington, we ran out of gas and called his grandfather who sent us gas. We dropped Alice off and took his grandfather's car for the rest of the evening. It had taken so long to get the gas that the restaurant was closed, and we got to Camp Leach after the meeting was over.

On the way back down that dark road from Camp Leach, we had a blow out. Man was it was dark, and I'm thinking, my mother let me out for this? A few minutes later a car came by and gave us enough light and help to get the tire changed. We sat there in the dark, probably both thinking it was time to eat since we had missed supper, but then something changed my heart. This guy, who seemed to have one problem after another and who must have been so embarrassed at the turn of events, was still smiling. This was the beginning of our courtship, November 21, 1957. I was a sophomore in high school, and he was a freshman at the University of North Carolina.

Since Bryan didn't have a car at school and had to hitchhike home to visit me on the weekends, we used my daddy's car. For fun, we'd see a movie and then go get a burger and shake. One time though, we decided to buy a Chef Boyardee pizza. Bryan said he had seen pizza in Chapel Hill, so with my cook's blood flowing, I couldn't wait to try this new dish.

Into the oven it went, and as the smell began to waft from the kitchen into other parts of our house, my parent's bedroom door flew open and out bolted my daddy in his underwear, and he started putting up the windows in the kitchen. He said never to cook anything else in his house that smelled like a dead rat. I guess the Parmesan cheese in the little can was more than his Southern nostrils could stand. It was some time before we actually had a pizza parlor in Greenville, but a few of the restaurants were beginning to serve pizza by my junior year in high school. Daddy never did develop a fondness for pizza and, like mushrooms, never found a home on his plate.

By the time I was a senior in high school, I knew I was in love for the rest of my life. Bryan worked in an awfully smelly pepper packing plant all summer to buy me a ring. I entered my senior year in high school engaged. I still planned to go to college and had been offered scholarships at Duke, University of North Carolina, East Carolina, and Cornell. My heart ruled, and I decided to attend the University of North Carolina Pharmacy School. After all, pharmacy has to be somewhat like cooking, a lot of ingredients being mixed up, following a formula.

Goodness and Grace

One evening, my friend Alice and I were going to a basketball game, and on 10th Street in Greenville, a car pulled out in front of me and suddenly stopped. Our fenders met with a bang and when I got out, there in the street was one of the fender guards off the front of Daddy's 1954 Pontiac. I was terribly upset as this was the first time I had been allowed to take the car out after dark, and I hadn't been away from home twenty minutes. The man driving the car said it was his fault and no damage had been done to his car, but I didn't feel any better so I turned around and went back home. Daddy had gone down the street to visit the Dails, and when I went in holding the fender guard and crying, he looked at me and said, "Is that all that's left?"
He took the fender guard and sent us back to the game. He had it put back on the next day and never mentioned it to me again. How forgiving, like our Father in Heaven. When our sins are forgiven, they are remembered no more. What an example my daddy was!

And Bryan was right there on campus. During my senior year, I was awarded Betty Crocker Homemaker of the Year, presented by General Mills. This, I thought, was very fitting since Betty Crocker had been by my side for years.

Chapel Hill

In the fall of 1960, I was a freshman at the University of North Carolina in Chapel Hill. It was awful. I was put in a women's dormitory with closed study every evening. We had inspection of our personal belongings. We had to eat that terrible food served in the dorm dining hall. We had to sign in and out. I thought I had become incarcerated and didn't know what crime I had committed except that I was a woman on a man's campus. And to top it off, we couldn't wear our Bermudas on campus unless we wore a raincoat over them, even if we were going to gym. What a double standard! I was ready to leave. Because I had a scholarship,

I was not allowed a car. Since I had always worked, I had always had a car. Bryan was on a scholarship and he couldn't have a car either, so we had to walk everywhere we went. I hated the whole scene.

We discovered that married couples have a little more freedom, even more so if you lived off campus. Without a lot of forethought, we eloped in a borrowed car and were married on January 18, 1961, in the First Baptist Church in Hillsborough, North Carolina. After we were married we had to hurry to get the car back. Then we walked down to the Rathskeller in downtown Chapel Hill, had a rare roast beef sandwich and a mug of iced tea. We both then went back to our dorms to study because exams started the next day.

Three days later, I was summoned to the Dean of Women's office. The pastor that married us turned us in to the school. Now that I was married, I would have to move out of the dorm, but Bryan would not. Talk about inequality!!!! This meant we had to call our parents. Fortunately, the world didn't end there, and we rented a 8×28-foot trailer close to school, were able to have a car, and things went on. Bryan graduated four months later and was accepted into law school.

The next fall, I became sick from eating too many oranges while trying to satisfy an uncontrollable craving and discovered the recovery time for my "illness" was nine months. We decided to have my family doctor, Dr. Brooks, deliver our baby, so several weeks before I was due, I went to stay with my parents. When labor pains started, I called Bryan, who was in Chapel Hill, and my friend Alice, who still lived down the street but was attending East Carolina, and she came to time my pains. Bryan made it in time, and our son Bryan Grimes III was born at 5:20 a.m. on May 10, 1962, weighing seven pounds, five ounces. I can say, in all honesty, B.G. was a beautiful baby, but he never slept a whole night through until he started school.

Take Offs and Landings

Bryan decided leave school for the United States Air Force as the war with Vietnam was heating up. We spent time at Biloxi AFB in Mississippi and McGuire AFB in New Jersey. While we were at McGuire, B.G. loved to go with his daddy to watch the planes land and take off. He liked to go with me to the base and make ceramics, and he especially liked painting them.

Much happened during the years 1963–1967. We lost a baby that would have been fourteen months younger than B.G. We were exposed to a lot of new situations because neither of us had been a lot of places. While we lived in New Jersey, I got a job writing feature stories for the Philadelphia Inquirer's New Jersey section and interviewed many interesting people in the area.

I also worked in a diner that made me appreciate foods other than our Southern fare. It was run by a Greek family, so we had homemade Greek dishes as well as absolutely wonderful Italian food. I learned a lot about kosher foods, and since I didn't know one single Jewish person growing up, I had never heard of lox and bagels.

They had their own baker there who would come in at night and bake the most wonderful desserts. If it had not been for B.G.'s being small, I would have wanted to work nights so I could get back in the bakery. As it was, I worked five hours in the evening, after Bryan got home, but I did get to smell some of the goodies before I came home in the evenings. I was still addicted to cooking, and while we lived in New Jersey, I entered several items in the culinary division of the state fair and won four blue ribbons, one being for the exquisite coconut cake, and I've included the recipe in the Family Favorites section.

We were at McGuire AFB until Bryan was sent to Vietnam. While he was overseas, B.G. and I went home to stay with my parents. We had seen many of our friends leave and not return home, and he did not want me on base away from home if something happened to him. It was a sad time for B.G., who was not quite three and loved his daddy dearly. He cried for his daddy for months, and my daddy would take him with him to try to take his mind off Bryan being gone. Every time B.G. saw a plane though, he would cry. It was during that time that B.G. and my daddy developed a very close and special relationship.

During the seemingly endless separation, B.G. and my daddy were out riding one day. My daddy has always carried cold drinks and snacks wherever he went. B.G. stuck his finger down his throat and turned to Daddy and said, "I stuck my finger down my throat and found out I was thirsty." My daddy recounted this story numerous times over the years, and he and B.G. always got a laugh out of it.

B.G. also spent a lot of time in the yard with Daddy that summer. It seemed that every time he went in the yard, a sparrow would circle around his head. One day it landed on his shoulder. From that day on until we left, every time he went outside, that little sparrow would sit on his shoulder, even when he was on the swing set. God knew B.G. was lonely for his Dad and that little bird was a comfort to him. When Bryan returned home, B.G. didn't want to have anything to do with him for a long time; he felt his dad had deserted him. After the tour of duty in Vietnam, Bryan decided to leave the USAF when his four years were up, and in 1967 he left as a first lieutenant.

You will notice that there has not been any mention lately about our spiritual life. We did attend church while we were in college but did not read the Word, or pray together, or even discuss God between the two of us. When we were in the service, it seemed our life was so full that on the weekends we didn't have time to seek out a church or even think about where we were going spiritually.

In 1967, we were back in North Carolina with Bryan working for the State of North Carolina, and as things began to settle down, we started attending church again. Our school days were over, our Air Force days were over, and we were about to begin the rest of our life.

For the Lord is good; his mercy is everlasting; and his truth endureth to all generations.

Psalms 100:5

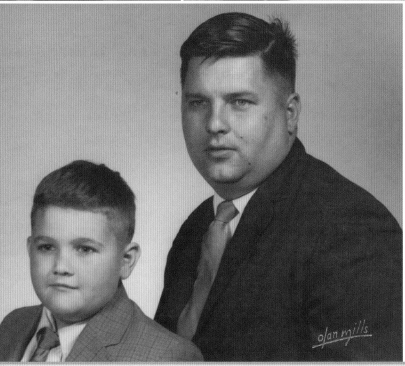

How good it was to be back in North Carolina, close to family. Bryan was working in Goldsboro, and we built a home in Grantham. I went to work with Mount Olive Pickle Company in data processing, and B.G., our son, was in grammar school. Two years later, Bryan had a chance to work with Pitt Tech, now Pitt Community College, so we moved to Winterville. I worked with Kroger during this time. We both wanted to have some kind of business, and an opportunity came up to open a Convenient Food Mart franchise in Southport. With some borrowed capital and a few passing prayers we embarked on our first entrepreneurial adventure.

Work became our life, as we were open seven days a week from 6 a.m. to midnight. Bryan's brother Bob moved to Southport to work with us, but the hours were still grueling and we had little life outside the business. We began attending the Episcopal Church there, and our rector told us we'd be just as well off sleeping on Sunday morning as coming to church, and I can say I'd agree with him on that, as the spiritual food being dished out in the mini sermon each Sunday would have resulted in spiritual starvation.

I remember one weekend my parents came to visit us. I had a big ham cooking in the oven and had made a big sheet pan of homemade rolls. B.G. was home with my parents, and I told them when the ham was ready to take it out. We all know that a ham is best when it's still warm and the juices from the fat are still running. Well, Bryan and I were about three hours late getting home from the Convenient Mart because someone didn't show up for work, and when we got home we had an empty pan with nothing but bones left. My daddy and our son had been eating all afternoon. Talking about going "whole hog."

We were in Southport for six years, and during that time, we opened a day care center as well as a bakery. It was a flourishing time for that small waterfront community, as they were building a nuclear reactor plant there as well as a Pfizer pharmaceutical plant. Suddenly the bubble burst when the decision was made not to build another reactor plant there. Construction workers left the area in droves, leaving homes vacant and business plummeting.

We had a spacious lovely home, a fishing boat, and a stressed life. Without God, there is no peace and joy, and we were certainly lacking that. One day, Bryan was approached by a man who began to question him about his spiritual life. As Bryan kept mulling over and over our

dry spiritual years, he remembered that when he was nine years old, his family life was so full of alcohol, screaming, and fighting that he cried out to God. Suddenly he was praying, not understanding the words, and yet he was understanding, and such a peace came over him. He recounted to me numerous times about experiencing God's awesome presence at a young age.

About the time Bryan was realizing that we both needed more of God in our lives, Mother sent us some books in the mail. There was a book by John Sherrill, a few by Oral Roberts, and one by Dennis Bennett. Bryan attended a Full Gospel Businessmen's meeting given by a lawyer on how God had turned his life around. By this time, God definitely had Bryan's attention, and while I worked that evening, he went to Wilmington. When he got back home late that night, he came to the side of the bed, woke me up, and said, "You're not number one in my life anymore." Although there had never been any problem with his straying, I realized he had been out much later than a normal meeting would have lasted (but I didn't know about Pentecostal prayer meetings), and now he was telling me this. I became very angry and demanded to know what he had been doing all evening.

He took my hand and in a calm voice said, "Jesus is number one in my life." While that settled that, it didn't make me feel any better. For some reason, I was still angry, at him, at my mother for sending those books that he had kept wanting me to read, at those crazy folks that kept him out all night, at God, at everything. Unexplainable anger that came from somewhere, possibly because I was not God to him anymore, that I was not on the pedestal that he had put me on, that he had moved onto something that was exciting to him and I had been left behind, although the choice had been mine. My ego was shattered, and for me to follow along just wasn't going to happen.

We began to see that business was not going to recover in the area anytime soon, so we put everything up for sale and moved closer to home. Just as we were getting settled in Rocky Mount, Mother had a stroke and was in a coma, and it looked like Daddy was going to need help when they released her to come home. We decided to make one more move back to Greenville. Just as we were getting ready to move, she died, but we had already gotten jobs in Greenville. Bryan was managing the parking lots at Pitt County Memorial Hospital, and I was the bakery manager at Krogers. The sequence of events and the timing of all this, the unlikelihood of these jobs just waiting for us had to be God.

We moved into a rental house right across from where I was born. At that time, we had five jobs between us. Our businesses and home in Southport had not sold, and we were still making payments. Over the next eighteen months, we were relieved of that debt.

We bought a lovely home on the other side of town, much smaller than the one we left in Southport, but God's hand worked it out that it was close to East Carolina University, where B.G. would be attending, and not too far from either of our jobs; now we had one job each.

We lived there from 1979 to 1985. In the meantime, God was out there directing, shifting, rearranging, and preparing. Bryan had continued with his Full Gospel meetings when we moved to Greenville, but I always had an excuse for not going. We had been going to a Free Will Baptist church with Daddy since

Mother died, and we were also going to the early communion service at the Episcopal church on Sunday mornings, so I thought that was enough—at least we were going to church. Bryan was still telling me I was missing so much by not allowing myself to experience what he had, and I kept telling him I was OK. Deep down though, I knew I was not OK.

While my mind accepted all Bryan was telling me, I still was not able to follow after him in that deeper walk. In my heart I knew he was right, and I needed that Baptism of the Holy Spirit, but my ego was still at odds with my heart. When the air cleared after Mother's death, I began to read the books she had been sending us. By the time we moved into our house that God so graciously provided through the sale of our businesses and our new jobs, I was seeking Him but had not resolved some issues in my mind.

One night when Bryan went to a Full Gospel Businessmen's meeting, I was home alone watching the PTL club. A lady was brought up on a cot to be prayed for. When they began to pray for her and she stood up and began to walk, I began to sing praises to God and a heavenly language began to come forth. I was still praising God when Bryan returned home. He came in the room and stood there listening to me, his face awash in tears. God is faithful and does answer prayers as he answered this one for Bryan.

Teach me to do thy will; for thou art my God; thy spirit is good; lead me into the land of uprightness.

Psalms 143:10

A New Day

We continued with our jobs and B.G., after graduating from Rose High School, enrolled at East Carolina University as a business major. I was still praying for another business. I preferred not to work retail and had prayed that if there was something I could do at home for God to show me.

One day at work I was decorating a cake and suddenly had a vision of a rolling pin rolling out dough. While it registered in my brain, it didn't have any significance to me. Two more times this vision came to me, and suddenly I said to myself, God wants me to start another bakery. Just like that, I decided this was what God wanted me to do. When I began to make inquiries, it seemed that all the doors were open and within a matter of months, I had opened a bakery beside the Harris Supermarket on Memorial Drive called the Rolling Pin.

While it was easy getting started, it seemed from the onset we had one problem after another. It seemed one piece of equipment after another needed repair. Every other day the bakery would be flooded, either from the laundromat next door where a washer had overflowed or the drains from the supermarket would be clogged up and water seeped in from under the walls. We couldn't work sloshing around in water, and it became frustrating trying to work around that.

We had quite a few wholesale customers, such as the grocery store next door, that were buying bread products and small cakes for resale. I also made rolls for several restaurants. Our sour cream and carrot cake donuts were very popular, and we were also making muffins and pita bread.

Our customers seemed to be pleased about our product line, except for three old ladies who started coming in two or three times a week asking if I made pastry. To us eastern North Carolinians, pastry is thin strips of dough boiled in chicken broth, commonly called chicken pastry here but probably better known as chicken and dumplings. I always told them no, and they kept saying that I needed to make it. One morning they came in and asked again. Before I could answer, one of them said to the others, "The reason she doesn't make it is she doesn't know how."

After they left, I kept hearing her say that over and over again. I thought, I haven't made pastry but a few times since I've been married and haven't had any since Mother died. Suddenly it seemed so important to see if I could make pastry, so like my socks were on fire, I hauled off to the back room and started measuring flour.

I made up a batch and then wondered how I was supposed to sell it. It would spoil in the bakery case, so I decided to pack it in some square aluminum pans I sold cakes in. I weighed out two pounds for each box and had enough for four boxes. I put it in a small ice cream case we had up front. Later that afternoon, those three ladies came again and said, "We want to buy some pastry."

Only God and I knew I had pastry. I sold each of them a box for $2, which left me one box. The next morning a lady came in and asked if I made pastry, and I sold her my last box. The thought occurred to me that maybe I did need to sell pastry, so I made up another batch and put a sign in the window. Within a few weeks, it was getting to be a chore rolling out all that dough, and one afternoon as I was rolling away and muttering about it, suddenly I remembered the vision of the rolling pin that landed me here in the bakery. "Oh no God, not this. This will kill me." I heard a voice say, "You know there's a machine that can do this." I did know about sheeters, but who would have thought I would sell so much pastry I would need a machine?

Suddenly it dawned on me that it had been a while since I had seen those old ladies; I wanted to ask them how they enjoyed the pastry. After a few days of wondering about them, I saw a grocery clerk outside and decided to ask him about the three old ladies in the blue car with the crumpled fender. He said he hadn't seen them; in fact, he said he had never seen them. I knew they must have shopped at the grocery store because they were here two or three times a week. To this day, I have never seen them again. Angels? I believe so. Sometimes if we are on the wrong path, God sends encouragement and he certainly baited me with the challenge of not knowing how to make pastry. We talk about how God provides and opens doors and such, but when you don't pray and find out first if that is what God has in mind for you, Satan will open the doors, hoping you will walk right through into his territory. He will do anything to keep God's perfect will for your life from ever coming into fruition.

One day a friend of ours came in after the Full Gospel Businessmen's breakfast, and I was telling him about my dilemma of selling the pastry and needing a piece of equipment that just wasn't in the budget. He said let's pray about this, and we did. He started out the door and then turned around and said for me to find the machine and he would buy it, lease it back to us, and when the last lease payment was made, it would be ours. Within a few weeks, the equipment was there, and we were making pastry. We still have that lease on the wall in our office and thank God for Charlie and his obedience to God.

We did not have room for the sheeter in back and had to set it up front behind the counter. Customers would come in and watch us make the pastry. Bryan was a salesman persona and convinced several grocery stores to carry the pastry. One day God spoke to me about not making any more pies and cakes. Then it was doughnuts. Then it was bread. I was beginning to get the message; it looked like pastry was to be the only thing we were to make. Then I heard him say, close the shop and go home. That's what we did. This was August 1981.

We turned our carport into an inspected bakery and only made pastry. Before we even turned out the first box of pastry at our home location, God spoke to me about putting a scripture verse in each box and that our commission was to feed physically and spiritually. We named our company Harvest Time Foods and even put in a prayer line. At the bottom of each scripture verse that we enclosed in each package was a number to call for prayer.

Business was growing supernaturally, and Bryan needed more time to sell so he resigned. With God leading and a super salesman like Bryan, we were selling all we could make. I hired two ladies to help, and one, Mary, is still working with us after almost twenty-six years. Jenny has been with us seventeen years.

Our son, B.G., has been a right arm in the business from its inception and has worked diligently at every task that came his way. His daddy and I have been so proud over the years of the long hours and hard work he has put into helping make Harvest Time Foods what it is today. He took a year off from East Carolina University to help out. Sales were spiraling, and soon it became necessary to go from Bryan's delivering directly to each store to warehouse distribution.

In less than a year, we were running out of room and moved to a small building on Highway 43 South. Within two years we needed more room and bought a building on the Old Tar Road that had once been the Tar Heel II, a notorious bar, where the sheriff's deputies spent quite a lot of time. After we remodeled the building and began operation there, it was not unusual to have someone banging on the door to get in for a beer. We did not have a company name up outside at that time but posted a sign that said, WE DO NOT SELL BEER. WE MAKE DOUGH. Then we would get folks who wanted to borrow money.

We were busy, but God had our attention. We were faithful in church, and God had laid on our hearts to be givers. We discovered as we gave, he was quick to replenish.

We found that we could not out-give God. Our needs were not always monetary needs, and God was always exceedingly generous in giving us favor with man.

In 1985, we moved from Greenville to a doublewide on the river while B.G. lived in our house in town to be close to the university. Soon, driving every day became a chore, so we thought we would build a house close to the plant. We purchased an eleven-acre tract about one-half mile away. We were also rapidly outgrowing our plant space and had plans drawn up to expand. However, the plans were not approved because of future widening of the

The Bible says in Luke 6:38, "Give, and it shall be given unto you; good measure, pressed down, and shaken together, and running over, shall men give into your bosom. For with the same measure that ye mete withal it shall be measured to you again."

road we were on. We went out to the eleven acres we had bought to build on and started building a new facility that was completed in January 1990. This denial of a building permit was a door God closed. We never could have expanded like we have needed to on the Tar Road Site.

In 1992, Harvest Time Foods was selected by Entrepreneur Magazine to receive the L.E.A.P. Award. This was for Leadership in Entrepreneurial Achievement and Philanthropy. We also were featured in Entrepreneur magazine in April of that year. Entrepreneurial Woman featured our company in the May issue with special emphasis on the company's generosity to the needy. That same year, our company was the North Carolina Small Business of the Year and was recognized as the U.S. Small Business Administration's Region IV small business of the year.

Recognition for a job well done is great, but how we view success is not always the way the world views it. As we grew, we knew that it had to be due to God, as we saw over and over again divine appointments. People would show up on our doorstep with just what we needed and didn't know where to look for it. Sometimes we would be shown items that we didn't need then, but within a short time we had a need for them. God knows the beginning from the end. He was and still is, as we are obedient to His calling, walking along beside us, giving us wisdom, and providing us the means to be a help to others.

As we began to expand our market even more, we began to market Anne's Chicken Base, a full-bodied paste containing little fat that would enhance not only chicken dishes but also could be used to season vegetables. Later we added Anne's Naturally Good Capsicana Sauce, a sweet and spicy sauce that complements any meat.

We began to work on our food service business and have developed a good following in the restaurant and institutional markets. Through the years, we have found that none of us can do it alone. Teamwork gets the job done—we have found partnering with our North Carolina Division of Marketing has helped us tremendously over the years and provided contacts that would have been difficult to make on our own. Our Goodness Grows and Flavors of Carolina programs are second to none in what they offer state food businesses, and we thank them for their ongoing efforts in promoting North Carolina products not only in our state, but throughout the United States.

We began to work consumer shows produced by Southern Shows based in Charlotte. These are first-class shows, and they have given us much exposure for our products by bringing us face-to-face with our customers and potential customers.

Bryan saw these shows as an opportunity to win lost souls, and as we were dishing out chicken and dumplings in our booth, he was presenting life everlasting to electricians, concession stand workers, exhibitors, and anyone who would listen. Seldom did we return from a show that two or three lost souls had not received salvation. He was tireless in his evangelistic endeavors.

In 1992, a wind blew into our life, not another hurricane Hazel, but Windy L. Johnson. B.G.'s personal life had been in a holding pattern as he finished his days at East Carolina with a degree in accounting and worked long hours with us in the business. A mutual friend set up a blind date, and his life has never been the same. Met in October, engaged in December, married in January, and now almost fourteen years later and with an eleven-year-old daughter, it's still Windy. She has been a helpmate for B.G. and a powerful prayer warrior.

And The Wind Blew In

I became acquainted with Harvest Time Foods while working with Johnston County Mental Health's Willie M. Program. I worked at a group home for adolescents, and we used to buy Anne's Old Fashioned Flat Dumplings to cook for the children. I enjoyed the product very much, especially the fact that they put scripture in every box and Jesus is Lord is on the outside of their boxes. I began praying for the company and putting the scriptures on the bulletin board for the kids to read. They enjoyed seeing what new scriptures would be up when we had dumplings. I did not know the family personally nor did I know that in the future that would change.

I became a Christian when I was sixteen years old and had served the Lord in various ways. I was involved in a women's ministry in Smithfield, North Carolina, known as Women's Aglow. It was in this ministry that I grew immensely in my relationship with the Lord. It was also in this ministry that I would meet a gentleman who would be very instrumental in introducing me to my future husband. Jim Lafferty said he knew a young man who would be perfect for me. Well, I was enjoying serving the Lord as a single adult, and I wasn't ready for a serious relationship at that time. I was also not too keen about blind dates. About a year later, I began to wonder if this young man had gotten married. I discovered that he had not. Jim gave the young man my name, address, and phone number.

It was not long before I received a call from him, and we became friends. We communicated several times by phone and had our first date in October 1992. We got married January 13, 1993. Jim was right; he was the perfect match for me. I guess you're saying to yourself, big deal, so you got married. I discovered during this time how much God has a sense of humor. The young man that Jim introduced me to was Bryan Grimes III, son of the owners of Harvest Time Foods. Little did I know during all those years of praying for the business to be blessed that I would be a part of the business. Now, that's just like my Jesus!

I prayed for years that when I married, my mother-in-law would be like a second mother to me and I would be like a daughter to her. Well, God answered our requests, for she had been praying for a daughter. Once again, we experienced God's faithfulness. All my previous jobs and ministry *opportunities prepared me for my various duties in the business. It is amazing how God in His mercy prepares us for what is ahead, even when we don't realize it at the time. Even when those tasks for which we have not had any prior experience are hard, his grace is sufficient.*

God is ever stretching us out of our comfort zone to be more conformed into His image. Sometimes during that stretching period, we go through a desert place, the very dry places in our lives. I know I went through a desert place for a period of time during the first year of marriage. But I discovered that it is in those dry places that we find out what our relationship with God is like. If we continue to seek him rather than despise the dry places, we will find out that He provides the living water that quenches the thirst of a parched soul and brings strength and comfort to a weary heart. Our Father loves to watch us grow, and he always provides what is essential to make us healthy and fruitful.

Although Harvest Time Foods is a small business, there is always plenty of action; it is never boring. Because we have collectively chosen to take a stand for Jesus, we come under a lot of spiritual attacks. Satan never takes a vacation, and he loves to use Christians as a part of his fun and amusement. We constantly have to stay on our toes by putting on the full armor of God. We have to make a daily decision to work as a unit. Satan loves to divide, and it takes wisdom and discernment to expose tactics that he may use to break our unity. I'm not implying that we do not get along; we do, but it's a choice we make. Doing God's will in each of our lives is more important than being right all the time or having our way all the time. We choose to walk in love and forgiveness; that's the only way we can be effective for His kingdom.

We strive to make a quality product and provide encouragement by putting scriptures on each box. We desire to make a difference in a world that needs Jesus and to glorify God while doing it. All we want in return is to hear Him say, 'Well done, my good and faithful servant." I am honored that God would give me the privilege of being a small part in this ministry, and being a part of the family is an extra bonus and blessing. God will indeed give us the desires of our heart if we will diligently seek Him and follow His commands. I know, for I have experienced it firsthand, and it gets better as the days go by. I am glad I am on the winning team; there is no place safer than being in the will of God and being led by His spirit.— *Windy Grimes*

WENDY'S INTERNATIONAL, INC.

R. DAVID THOMAS

Senior Chairman of the Board & Founder

April 1, 1992

Mr. & Mrs. Bryan Grimes
Harvest Time Foods
P.O. Box 98
Ayden, NC 28513

Dear Anne and Bryan:

I enjoyed meeting you last week in New York. Congratulations on receiving MasterCard's regional L.E.A.P. Award. It is a tribute to your skills as entrepreneurs and to your generosity as a corporate citizen.

I certainly understand the trials and tribulations that go with owning and operating a business. I also remember how motivating it is to be recognized for your hard work and persistence. To me, though, one of the most important elements of success is the ability to give something back to the community that supports you. Your fundraising work for food banks and children's charities is highly commendable and will undoubtedly touch the lives of many people in need.

Anne and Bryan, you should be very proud of what you have accomplished, and I wish you many, many more years of success.

Sincerely,

R. David Thomas

4288 WEST DUBLIN GRANVILLE ROAD, D

Goodness Grows in North Carolina

Hall Of Fame

nne Grimes

arvest Time Foods

1994

Mildred Anne Grimes
Owner
Harvest Time Foods
Ayden, North Carolina

W
I
N
N
E
R

rimes, Jr.
wner
ime Foods
th Carolina

NAEGELE

The Chamber *Recognizes its members...*

Linda Thompson - Hank's Homemade Ice Cream
1992 Pitt County Small Business Leader of the Year

Bryan & Anne Grimes - Harvest Time Foods
1992 SBA N.C. Small Business Leaders of the Year
1992 SBA Southeastern United States
Small Business Leaders of the Year

Pitt-Greenville Chamber of Commerce, Inc.

SMALL BUSINESS WEEK
U.S. Small Business Administration

Goodness Grows in North Carolina
1994 Awards Recipients

The 1994 Goodness Grows in North Carolina Hall of Fame inductee was Mrs. Anne Grimes of Harvest Time Foods, Ayden, North Carolina. Pictured here with Mrs. Grimes are (l to r) Commissioner Jim Graham, Director of Marketing M. Wayne Miller, and Warron Williams.

PERDUE

Anne Grimes,
n one of her loyal customers,
Mitzi Perdue
Frank Perdue

ANNE'S

LET
ANNE'S
DOUGH
WORK
FOR YOU
IN '91

HAM

In the fall of 1994, a new team member, Cathy, joined us as a sales manager. As I took my first trip with her, I would have never thought it would have been so exciting. I picked her up in Charlotte to go to Birmingham where we were to attend a Flavors of Carolina show. As we rode along getting to know one another better, we saw it getting a little cloudy, but nothing to be concerned about. We stopped for a break and came out of the gas station noting it had really gotten dark.

We headed on toward Birmingham and suddenly we saw large towers of lightning that went from the ground to the sky, the wind began to blow, and it started hailing. What we didn't know was that we were under a tornado as we came into Birmingham. It was raining so hard we missed our turnoff to the hotel, which was a blessing from God. The tornado went right down the street where we were supposed to turn and did a terrific amount of damage in the block next to our hotel. When we finally got to the hotel everyone came running out to see if we had had any problems, telling us about the tornado. This storm killed quite a few people in its path, and we were right under it.

We have had a lot of exciting adventures since then which would take another book to recount.

I must tell you about Elizabeth Anne. I attended a doctor's appointment with Windy when she was about four weeks shy of her delivery date. As I waited for her, a nurse ran up to me, saying they were admitting Windy to the hospital for delivery. I thought she was in labor, but it was more critical than that. Her placenta had separated, and the baby was not getting nourishment.

The doctor performed a Caesarean and a little after 4 a.m. on July 13, 1995, Elizabeth Anne Grimes was born, weighing just two pounds, six ounces. We all prayed for her in the neonatal unit because she was so small. Windy herself was so ill with toxemia that we nearly lost her. She did not get to see "Beth Anne" for three days after the birth.

Beth Anne grew and thrived even though she has had some health problems. And once she found the start button, she has never stopped talking. She is a joy to me as she was to her granddaddy.

Bryan's Song

About this time, we began to realize that my husband Bryan had some medical problems. In 1992, he had a rash on his stomach that turned into a bullseye before I could drag him to the doctor. He had a tick bite and received antibiotics, but it had already been there a month. Two weeks later, he got up one morning looking like a monster out of a horror movie. The doctor said he had Bells Palsy and gave him a steroid.

He was very sick for three weeks with flu-like symptoms, and when he recovered he seemed so tired. From then on, it seemed about every six to eight weeks he would have some type of neurological situation that would cause him to slur his speech, forget things, and drag his feet. The doctor now said he was having mini strokes. His blood pressure was elevated, but the blood pressure medication seemed to put everything in slow motion for him. He had absolutely no energy and was experiencing tremors. When it became apparent that he was not going to be able to function enough to continue working, in 1995, he passed on the presidency of Harvest Time Foods to B.G.

Though we were told these neurological episodes were attributable to strokes, I believed that he had Lyme disease. I bought every book that I could find and began using natural remedies. In 2004 we found a doctor who tested Bryan and said he did have Lyme disease, as well as two other tick-borne diseases. Diagnosis at that time gave us little hope for recovery, but hopefully we could maintain the current level of function. When he was put on a rotating antibiotic schedule, suddenly his blood pressure normalized, and he was able to give up his prescription medications.

While Bryan's condition was worsening with each passing year, I was given a prescription drug that caused my body to go haywire, and it seemed that I could not get my blood sugar or blood pressure to normalize. I felt that I couldn't continue to care for Bryan. The physical and mental drain was beginning to wear me out. In November 2002, I saw an advertisement in our local paper about a doctor who had perfected a procedure that would involve a minimally invasive surgery that was very effective at eradicating the kinds of problems that I was experiencing. I had also had low metabolism since I was in third grade, and I had taken medication most of my life but never seemed to be able to keep my weight under control, although I was not a big eater. I immediately felt this was my answer.

Bryan and I went to New Bern, North Carolina, to listen to Dr. Donald Rutledge and immediately I felt peace about this surgery called the mini gastric bypass. I scheduled surgery for January 26, 2003. Cathy drove us to Statesville, and we had a big snow the night after we arrived, causing the pre-op class held the day before surgery to be cancelled. By surgery day, even though it was pretty treacherous getting to the hospital from the motel, we made it safely, and within thirty-six minutes of entering surgery at 2:30, it was over. Within a few hours, I was up and walking. By ten o'clock the next morning, I was shopping in Wal Mart. I was on a liquid diet for a month, soft foods for another month and then began to add regular foods. I lost 139 pounds in fourteen months and am thankful to God for giving Dr. Rutledge the skill to perform this surgery and save my life. Had I not had this surgery, I would not have been able to care for Bryan those last four years and look forward to seeing my granddaughter grow up. I praise God for His deliverance from these diseases. I am healthy now, look younger, feel younger, and can keep up with the young folks.

Bryan had wanted to go to Israel for years, and in 2000, God made it possible for us to take that journey. We needed a caravan of camels to haul everything we needed to take for those ten days because we knew some items were not available there. With the wheelchair and all our belongings, we departed for that once-in-a-lifetime trip. We were both excited about the trip, but it would not have been possible without the help of our pastor Joseph and evangelist friend John. Little did they know just how much we were going to need them.

Bryan has always enjoyed a good laugh, even if it was on him. One evening we returned to the hotel late, and he needed a shower. We were just finishing up when he slipped and went down in the tub. It was a midget tub with a giant residing in it. He was wet and suction was created when he went down, so there was no way could I get him upright. A call at that late hour brought help, and because we were laughing over the situation, it was even harder to get him out. Bryan's only concern was that they have him out in time to catch the tour bus the next day.

A similar incident happened in 2005 while we were at Miracle Mountain in western North Carolina for a five-week series of hyperbaric oxygen treatments designed to improve the flow of oxygen to his brain. The Hartsoes, who started this wonderful facility, as well as their Christian staff, were so gracious to us during our stay. We took a motor home up there, but we still needed a regular bathroom and a washer and dryer. We rented half of a mobile home from them for Bryan to stay in. One weekend I was cooking supper when Bryan decided on a shower. Just as he was about to get out, down he went with almost the same situation as in Israel, except no Joseph or John. Everyone else had gone to town and we were "home alone." Why situations like this make you laugh, I don't know, but here was Bryan, stuck in the tub again. We were laughing and crying at the same time.

This was a serious predicament. I began to pray, and Bryan was getting cold so I threw towels on him. Then out of the blue a thought came: what about the aero bed in the motor home? Though I couldn't imagine what good it would do, I went out to get it anyway. When I got back in, after some false starts, I had an idea. I took one corner and raised one hip so I could slide it under and let some air in it. That side started to rise. I pushed some more of the bed under him and let some more air go in. About a dozen tries later, he was up high enough in the tub for me to roll him out onto the floor where I could use his gait belt to get him up. Did he say thank you? After all, this took about two hours of my working up a sweat. Nope. His question was, "When is supper?"

I have heard that what happens twice, happens three times, and I decided we would not stay away from home unless we could get a shower without a tub. I would hear Bryan sitting in his lift chair laughing and would ask him what was so funny, and he would say, "Rub-a dub, dub, one big man in a tub. A pull here. A pull there. Supper is near. I gotta get outta here!"

Bryan lost so many of his functions over the years, with triple bypass surgery in 2005, excessive bleeding in 2006, and progressive brain stem disease that caused dementia. We were able to maintain him at a sufficient level so that, with help, in May of 2006 we were able to take a five-day trip to the Bahamas. This was a special trip for us, and I'm sure he realized that it was probably the last big trip we could take. He collapsed the second day we were there, but his brother Demsie was there to help. He enjoyed all that he could do, which was mostly eating fabulous food, especially a crab cake he ate at the Seafire Steakhouse; he was still talking about it six months later.

Time also was running out for someone else that I loved dearly. Sister Becky always loved the water and some years ago moved to Manns Harbor, North Carolina. She lived at the end of a road that looked like the Florida Everglades. The fish were always biting in the waters off the end of her pier, and come rain or shine you would see fishing lines swaying in the wind at the end of the pier. She could watch them from her window and if she had some nibbles, she would hurry to the end of the pier and take a place there as long as the fish were biting. This was like Heaven to her, and neither I nor anyone else could convince her she didn't need to live down there alone. Her health deteriorated during 2006, and she died at the place she loved so much on June 29, at the age of 57. There was not a more generous nor kind person, and she will be missed. She was the chef par excellence of chocolate chess pies, and there is no doubt that with her passing QVC stock plummeted.

As 2006 progressed, it was apparent that the clock was running down for Bryan, too. His condition was getting worse, and in December, Bryan began to have headaches and experienced several mini strokes. On December 28, 2006, he suffered a massive brain stem stroke, and he passed from earth into the Heavenly realm on December 29. We miss him.

Life goes on. Bryan would not want us to be sad. He was excited about some things that were in the works before he died. He always wanted us to enjoy life, and when I was happy, he was happy. I had an opportunity in November to take a couple of days off with Cathy and go to Paula Deen's Cooking School. I would guess that if you've watched many cooking shows, you must know that she is the Southern Queen of cooking on the Food Network. I got to personally meet her and found out that she used our Anne's Flat Dumplings and had for years. When I passed that information on to Bryan his comment was, "I don't understand why you're so excited about meeting her. I bet she can't cook as good as you." Nevertheless, he was happy for me when Follow Productions called and said Paula wanted to have me on her Paula's Party show. Taping was scheduled for January 19, the day after what would have been our forty-sixth anniversary. Because of his condition, I was not going to be able to take him with me for the taping, but as it turned out, I'm sure he was right there.

> *When he was able, Bryan would speak this blessing from Numbers 6 over friends as they were leaving, and I now speak this over all of you.*
>
> *The Lord bless thee and keep thee.*
> *The Lord make His face to shine upon thee, and be gracious unto thee.*
> *The Lord lift up His countenance upon thee and give thee peace.*

A grandmother has a special place in her heart for her grandchildren, and my heart always skips a beat when I hear Beth Anne's voice. After her PaPa died, Beth Anne spent the first few weekends with me and was such a comfort to me; she'll never know how much. She is growing up quickly, and I know soon I'll have to compete for her time as her interests expand, but she'll always be special because she is who she is and my prayer for her is that she love the Lord and follow after Him with her whole heart for all of her days.

My other buddy, a soft, cuddly, feline fur ball named Beau, has been constantly at my feet.

He, too, misses that figure snoozing in the lift chair with his headphones on as South Pacific plays away. Pets, too, can grieve, and I know he knows things will never be the same.

Yes, these last years have been hard. Especially the first months of 2007. My best friend and soul mate is gone. I can't reach out to steady him as he falters or wipe the food off his chin, but forever he resides in my heart, still encouraging me with, "If that's what you want, do it." We did it together so long, and now that the struggling is over for him, I am envious that he is experiencing firsthand what our Lord Jesus has promised us.

> *To him that overcometh will I grant to sit with Me in My throne, even as I also overcame, and am set down with My Father in His throne.*
>
> **Revelation 3:21**

This is not my story, but the story of a family and the years that God has given us here, hopefully making a difference in the lives we touch each day. Every day is a gift from God, and it's what we do with it that counts. I rejoice that He is so loving and merciful and delivered me when I made bad choices. I did not deliberately look to follow after evil, but I did make choices that allowed Satan to lead me astray. I am so grateful for the prayers of the Saints and God's grace in answering them.

I can't end this without saying that any of you who have doubts that there is a true living God, understand that there is no way without His hand of protection that this story could be written, because I would not be here to write it. I wish God's best for each of you as you live each day for Him. He will reward you here on earth with peace and joy, and one day we, too, shall be seated in high places with Him.

Enter into his gates with Thanksgiving and into his courts with praise: be thankful unto him and bless his name. For the Lord is good; his mercy is everlasting and his truth endureth to all generations.

Psalms 100:4–5

God is constantly working behind the scenes on our behalf. If we could just somehow get a glimpse into his heart and know how much He really cares about our lives down to the smallest detail. He knows our needs before we know we have a need.

I will never truly understand why it was necessary for us to go through these last fourteen years with Bryan struggling with Lyme disease and its effects, but I do know there is a purpose for everything that happens to us. Neither of us ever blamed God, but we felt there was a higher purpose in all this and determined that as best we could, we would live as Godly examples of God's grace and mercy.

We know that He will never leave us nor forsake us, and He knew the time to call Bryan home. He has been my ever-present help in time of trouble, right here by my side during this time of grieving. Yes, it is okay to grieve.

Moving on is not easy, but God already had in place such wonderful supportive friends and family. He moved us into a loving, caring church fellowship almost four years ago, and they will never know how much the visits and phone calls meant to Bryan. While he may have fallen asleep during visits, it made him happy to know someone cared. Little things meant a lot to him.

For those of us who are mobile and able to freely communicate with each other, we sometimes overlook the small kindnesses that others do for us. Lyn and Brenda came into our lives, and I am so grateful for the bond that Bryan and Lyn had. I am thankful for the funny jokes and pictures that came our way via email that I was able to share with Bryan; the Sunday nights after church at Bojangles, with Gene cleaning his glasses after Bryan had eaten corn on the cob; Barbara sending love with her special cards and goodies. Pat and Tommy, our support people from afar, are truly God seekers.

Pat has a wonderful collection of Biblical pearls of wisdom that she agreed to let me make available to you in the chapter called Bread for the Journey. I call it Lagniappe, which means an extra or unexpected gift for you. It will stimulate your desire to be more like Him. My Aunt Elsie is always there, praying and encouraging. A heartfelt thanks to Sandy and Connie for their prayers and hospital visits, our neighbors, Pastor Brad, and our church family—what wonderful support groups; Linda, who has been a consistent prayer warrior for me; Howard and Wanda, who were so vigilant in making us comfortable after Bryan's death. I could go on and on. I can't mention everyone, but you know who you are. I pray for you all daily and thank you for your prayers in return.

As I was pulling out pictures from our albums, I came across a book of poems that I had written back in the 1960s. The first one that I saw was one called Eternity. It was like Bryan speaking to me, reassuring me that he was fine and I needed to move on in what God had for me to do now; he would be waiting for me when God called me. How wonderful that God would inspire me to write that poem in 1968, almost thirty-eight years ago for a time such as this, to encourage me. He knows the beginning from the end, and I shall praise His name forever.

Eternity

I watch you from my dimension,

Wishing you could see me.

How it would dry your tears

To see how happy I am.

But how could you ever know

Of the never ceasing wonders

In this plane of being.

Of free soul, free spirit

Of time everlasting,

Of ultimate fulfillment.

Strive now for a beautiful life.

Do not still grieve.

Someday soon you'll span the webbing of eternity,

And I'll clasp your hand,

Hold you close,

Welcoming you Home.

Harvest Time Recipes

Getting Started

Cooking has been a significant part of my life these sixty-five years, and I will tell you right up front, very few of the favorite recipes that you find in *Dumplings 'N More* came from the originator. Recipes are like hand-me-downs—getting passed down as long as there is any life left in them, so some of these recipes have been around for a long time.

Most of us, no matter how much we like a recipe, can't help but change an ingredient or two or add a dash of this or that. Suddenly we have our very own unique version of an old recipe, and it becomes Betty's pie or Joan's cake, and then we get requests for OUR recipes.

I have been blessed to have excellent cooks in my family who passed on some super-good recipes to me, as well as having been surrounded by those Saints whose covered dishes make your mouth water just thinking about them and friends who would show up on my doorstep with one of their out-of-this-world concoctions. I thank all of you who have kept my palate excited with new taste sensations over the years. So in reality, this is not MY cookbook, but I give credit to each of YOU who so graciously shared your culinary skills with me through the years in making this book possible.

Some recipes included here will mention an ingredient by brand name, but this does not imply endorsement of that brand over another—is it given to simplify the recipe. BUT, when you see Anne's products mentioned, that is an emphatic—Go Buy It. It Is the Best!

He that dwelleth in the secret place of the most High shall abide under the shadow of the Almighty. I will say of the Lord, He is my refuge and my fortress: my God; in him will I trust.
—Psalms 91:1-2

Old-Fashioned Chicken 'n Dumplings

1 large chicken
4 quarts water
Salt to taste
1 (24-ounce) package Anne's Flat Dumplings
Pepper to taste

Cook the chicken in 4 quarts salted water in a stockpot until tender and cooked through. Remove the chicken to a platter to cool, reserving the broth. Add enough water to the broth to measure 5 to 6 quarts and bring to a boil. Remove the chicken from the bones and discard the bones. Remove the dumplings from the freezer 5 minutes before cooking. Add eight to ten dumplings to the boiling broth and stir gently. Return the broth to a boil and add eight to ten more dumplings. Continue the process until all the dumplings have been added to the broth, stirring after each addition. Bring to a full boil and boil for 6 minutes, stirring frequently to keep the dumplings separated. Add the chicken and boil for 2 minutes. Remove the stockpot from the heat and let stand, covered, for 20 to 30 minutes before serving. Season to taste.

Serves 8 to 12

For easier separation of the dumpling layers, remove the dumplings from the box and microwave for 15 seconds. Any dumpling strips that are not used may be refrozen. For a heartier broth, add 2 tablespoons Anne's Chicken Base.

E-Z Chicken 'n Dumplings

4 quarts water
3 tablespoons Anne's Chicken Base
1/4 cup (1/2 stick) butter
1 (24-ounce) package Anne's Flat Dumplings
1 (12-ounce) can cooked chicken, drained
All-purpose flour (optional)
Salt and pepper to taste

Bring the water, chicken base and butter to a boil in a heavy 6-quart stockpot. Add five to seven dumplings and stir gently. Return the water to a boil and add five to seven more dumplings. Continue the process until all the dumplings have been added to the water, stirring after each addition. Add the chicken and boil for 8 to 10 minutes or until the dumplings are tender, stirring frequently to keep the dumplings separated. Add flour mixed with water to thicken the broth, if desired. Season with salt and pepper. Garnish with sliced hard-cooked eggs.

Serves 8 to 12

Chicken 'n Dumplings Soup

Bring 6 cups water and 2 tablespoons Anne's Chicken Base to a boil in a large stockpot. Cut 10 strips of Anne's Flat Dumplings into 1/2-inch-wide pieces. Add to the water and return to a boil. Boil for 8 to 10 minutes, stirring occasionally. Add 1 1/2 cups chopped cooked chicken and salt and pepper to taste. Boil for 2 minutes. You may use canned chicken, if desired. You also may add chopped onion and celery and grated carrots when you add the dumplings to the water.

Serves 6

Chicken Fricassee

1 (3-pound) chicken
3 tablespoons Anne's Chicken Base
1/4 cup chopped celery
1/4 cup chopped onion
Salt and pepper to taste
1/4 cup diced pimentos
1/4 cup all-purpose flour
1/4 cup water
Hot cooked rice or noodles

Cut the chicken into eight pieces. Combine the chicken with water to cover in a 4- to 6-quart pot. Add Anne's Chicken Base, the celery, onion, salt and pepper. Cook over medium heat until the chicken is tender and cooked through, stirring occasionally. Remove the chicken to a platter. Increase the heat and bring the stock to a boil. Boil until the stock is reduced to about 1 quart. Add the pimentos.

Combine the flour and 1/4 cup water in a small bowl and mix well. Stir into the boiling stock gradually. Boil until the stock thickens, stirring frequently. Arrange the chicken on a platter over rice or noodles. Pour the stock over the chicken.

Serves 6 to 8

Before roasting a turkey or chicken, rub the outside of the skin with a coating Anne's Chicken Base. Rub inside the cavity with 1 teaspoon Anne's Chicken Base. This will give your gravy a more full-bodied flavor.

Chicken and Dressing Casserole

1/2 cup (1 stick) butter, melted
1/2 cup water
1 tablespoon Anne's Chicken Base
2 sleeves saltine crackers, crushed
1/2 onion, minced
1/4 cup diced celery
1 (10-ounce) can cream of celery soup
1 (10-ounce) can cream of mushroom soup
3 eggs, beaten
3 cups chopped cooked chicken

Preheat the oven to 350 degrees. Combine the butter and water in a large bowl. Add Anne's Chicken Base and stir until dissolved. Add the crackers, onion, celery and soups and mix well. Stir in the eggs. Fold in the chicken. Spoon into a greased 9×13-inch baking dish. Bake for 35 to 40 minutes or until golden brown.

Serves 6 to 8

Barbecue Chicken

Place a chicken in a baking dish and bake at 350 degrees until cooked through and golden brown. Baste with Anne's Capsicana Sauce.

Serves 4

Anne's Capsicana Sauce is a versatile sauce that can be used as a dip for chilled cooked shrimp; as a sauce for beef, pork, chicken, baked salmon, or scrambled eggs; or as a dressing for salads.

Steak-umms Casserole

18 strips Anne's Flat Dumplings
2 quarts water
Salt to taste
1 (28-ounce) jar Prego spaghetti sauce or your favorite spaghetti sauce

1 onion, thinly sliced
$1/2$ green bell pepper, diced
$41/2$ frozen Steak-umms
4 ounces mozzarella cheese, shredded

Preheat the oven to 350 degrees. Add Anne's Flat Dumpling strips to 2 quarts boiling salted water. Boil for 3 minutes, stirring frequently; drain. Spoon a thin layer of spaghetti sauce over the bottom of a 9×9-inch baking pan. Top with six dumpling strips and one-third of the onion slices. Sprinkle with one-third of the bell pepper. Break up $11/2$ of the Steak-umms and arrange over the bell pepper. Repeat the layers twice. Sprinkle with the cheese. Bake for 50 to 55 minutes or until bubbly.

Serves 6

Skillet Beef 'n Dumplings

1 pound ground beef
$1/2$ cup chopped onion
$1/2$ cup chopped celery
1 (4-ounce) can sliced mushrooms
1 (10-ounce) can cream of mushroom soup
1 green bell pepper, chopped

1 (2-ounce) jar pimento
1 cup milk
1 tablespoon Worcestershire sauce
1 teaspoon salt
6 layers Anne's Flat Dumplings
$1/2$ cup (or more) water

Cook the ground beef, onion and celery in a large skillet over medium heat, stirring until the beef is brown and crumbly; drain. Stir in the undrained mushrooms, soup, bell pepper, pimento, milk, Worcestershire sauce and salt. Add Anne's Flat Dumplings and bring to a boil. Add the water and reduce the heat. Simmer, covered, for 25 minutes or until the dumplings are tender, stirring occasionally and adding more water if needed.

Serves 4

Country Ham 'n Dumplings

Boil a country ham bone or 3 pounds ham hocks in water to cover in a large stockpot until the meat is falling from the bone. Remove from the stock. Separate the meat from the bones and discard the bones. Add enough water to the stock to measure 3 quarts. Add eight layers of Anne's Flat Dumpling Strips to the stock and bring to a boil. Boil for 8 minutes, stirring occasionally. Return the ham to the stockpot. You may add cooked butter beans, corn and peas for variety, if desired.

Serves 6

Pork Backbone 'n Dumplings

Boil a 3- to 5-pound pork backbone in water to cover in a large stockpot until the meat is tender. Season to taste with salt and pepper. Remove the pork from the stockpot. Add enough water to the stock to measure 5 quarts and bring to a boil. Using a 24-ounce package of Anne's Flat Dumplings, add five to seven strips to the stockpot and stir gently. Return the stock to a boil and add five to seven more dumpling strips. Repeat the process until you have added all the dumplings, stirring after each addition. Cook for 8 to 10 minutes. Return the pork to the stockpot. Remove from the heat and let stand, covered, for 30 minutes.

Serves 8 to 12

Instead of adding butter to your mashed potatoes,
add 1 teaspoon Anne's Chicken Base, or more
or less to taste.

Pork Loin

1- to 3-pound boneless pork loin
Salt and pepper to taste

1/4 cup vinegar
1/2 cup Anne's Capsicana Sauce

Preheat the oven to 350 degrees. Place the pork loin in a baking dish and season with salt and pepper. Pour the vinegar over the pork. Bake until a meat thermometer inserted in the pork reads 150 degrees and the pork is tender and brown, basting occasionally with 1/4 cup of Anne's Capsicana Sauce. Just before removing the pork from the oven, combine the remaining 1/4 cup Anne's Capsicana Sauce with the pan drippings in a bowl and mix well. Pour over the pork. Let the pork cool for 15 to 20 minutes before serving.

Serves 6 to 8

Sausage 'n Dumplings Casserole

1 pound bulk pork sausage
1/2 cup chopped onion
1/4 cup chopped green bell pepper
1 (10-ounce) can cream of chicken soup
1/2 cup water

8 layers Anne's Flat Dumplings,
   cooked and drained
Salt and pepper to taste
1/2 cup crumbled French-fried onions

Preheat the oven to 350 degrees. Crumble the sausage into a large skillet. Add the onion and bell pepper and cook over medium heat until the sausage is brown and the vegetables are tender, stirring frequently; drain. Combine with the soup, water, Anne's Flat Dumplings, salt and pepper in a large bowl and mix well. Spoon into a greased 2-quart baking dish. Sprinkle with the crumbled onions. Bake for 30 minutes or until bubbly.

Serves 4 to 6

Oyster Fritters

1 tablespoon Anne's Chicken Base	1 sleeve saltine crackers, crushed
2 cups water	2 pints oysters, drained
1/2 cup (1 stick) butter	Vegetable oil
1 egg, well beaten	

Combine Anne's Chicken Base, the water, butter, egg, crackers and oysters in a bowl and mix well. Heat vegetable oil to 350 degrees in a large deep skillet over medium-high heat. Drop the oyster mixture by teaspoonfuls into the oil and cook until brown.

Serves 6 to 8

Alfredo Sauce with Dumplings

6 layers Anne's Flat Dumplings	1/4 cup milk
2 quarts water	1/4 cup (1 ounce) grated Parmesan cheese
Salt to taste	1 teaspoon Anne's Chicken Base
4 ounces cream cheese, softened	Garlic salt (optional)
1/4 cup (1/2 stick) butter, softened	

Combine Anne's Flat Dumplings with 2 quarts salted water in a large stockpot. Bring to a boil and boil for 8 to 10 minutes, stirring occasionally. Remove from the heat and let stand, covered, for 15 minutes; drain.

Place the cream cheese and butter in a double boiler set over simmering water. Add the milk, Parmesan cheese and Anne's Chicken Base and heat until thickened, stirring frequently. Add garlic salt to taste. Place the dumplings in a serving dish. Pour the Alfredo Sauce over the top and serve immediately.

Serves 4

Lasagna

Preheat the oven to 350 degrees. Cook nine layers of Anne's Flat Dumplings in boiling salted water in a large stockpot for 3 to 4 minutes. Drain and set aside. Spread a layer of marinara or meat sauce over the bottom of a 9×13-inch baking pan. Arrange a layer of nine dumplings over the sauce. Top with ricotta cheese. Repeat the layering process twice. Spread marinara or meat sauce over the top and sprinkle with shredded mozzarella cheese. Bake for 45 to 50 minutes or until bubbly.

Serves 8 to 12

Ravioli

Thaw five layers of Anne's Flat Dumplings. Place 1 teaspoon ravioli filling on one end of each dumpling. Fold the other end of the dumpling over to enclose the filling, crimping the edges to seal. Bring 2 quarts water and 1 teaspoon salt to a boil in a stockpot. Drop the ravioli into the boiling water and stir gently. Return to a boil and boil for 8 minutes; drain. Serve immediately with marinara sauce.

Serves 4

**Instead of adding butter to your rice, add 1 teaspoon
Anne's Chicken Base, or more or less to taste.**

Peas 'n Dumplings

4 quarts water	1/2 package Anne's Flat Dumpling Strips
2 tablespoons Anne's Chicken Base	1 quart fresh garden peas, cooked
3 tablespoons butter	Salt and pepper to taste

Bring the water to a boil in a large stockpot. Add Anne's Chicken Base and the butter. Drop five to seven Anne's Dumpling Strips into the boiling broth and stir gently. Return the broth to a boil and add five to seven more dumpling strips. Continue the process until all the dumpling strips have been added to the broth, stirring after each addition. Boil for 8 to 10 minutes, stirring occasionally. Add the peas and season with salt and pepper. Remove from the heat and let stand, covered, for 30 minutes.

Serves 6

Spinach 'n Dumplings Casserole

1 (10-ounce) package frozen leaf spinach, thawed and drained	1 1/2 cups milk
8 layers Anne's Flat Dumplings, cooked and drained	1 cup (4 ounces) shredded Cheddar cheese
3 eggs	2 cups ricotta cheese
	Salt and pepper to taste

Preheat the oven to 375 degrees. Spread the spinach over the bottom of a buttered 7×11-inch baking dish. Cover the spinach with the dumplings. Beat the eggs and milk in a bowl. Add the Cheddar cheese, ricotta cheese, salt and pepper and mix well. Pour over the dumplings. Bake for 35 to 45 minutes or until set.

Serves 6

Corn Chowder

1 quart water
2 tablespoons Anne's Chicken Base
2 to 3 potatoes, diced
1 onion, chopped
2 (15-ounce) cans whole kernel corn, drained
2 cups half-and-half
1/2 cup (1 stick) butter

Combine the water, Anne's Chicken Base, potatoes and onion in a large heavy stockpot. Bring to a boil and boil until the potatoes are tender. Add the corn, half-and-half and butter and return to a boil; reduce the heat. Simmer for about 5 minutes. Season to taste.

Serves 6

Add 1 tablespoon Anne's Chicken Base to a pot of collards, cabbage, greens, or string beans instead of meat seasoning.

Anne's Potato Soup

4 green onions, chopped
1 stalk celery, finely chopped
1/4 cup (1/2 stick) butter
4 potatoes, diced
2 tablespoons Anne's Chicken Base

4 cups water
1 teaspoon salt (optional)
1/2 teaspoon pepper (optional)
1 (5-ounce) can evaporated milk

Sauté the green onions and celery in the butter in a skillet until translucent or microwave in a microwave-safe dish until translucent. Combine the potatoes, Anne's Chicken Base, water, salt and pepper in a saucepan and bring to a boil. Add the celery mixture. Reduce the heat and simmer until the potatoes are cooked through, stirring occasionally. Add the evaporated milk and simmer for 5 minutes, stirring occasionally.

Serves 6 to 8

Capsicana Dip

4 ounces cream cheese, softened
3 tablespoons mayonnaise
1/4 cup Anne's Capsicana Sauce
1 small onion, diced

Combine the cream cheese, mayonnaise, Anne's Capsicana Sauce and the onion in a bowl and mix well. Chill until serving time. Serve with crackers.

Makes about 1 cup

Baked Pastry Strips

Preheat the oven to 425 degrees. Place Anne's Flat Dumpling Strips on a baking sheet. Sprinkle with salt. Bake until light brown. These are eaten like crackers with chicken pastry (the Eastern North Carolina name for chicken and dumplings).

OTHER OPTIONS

Sprinkle sesame seeds or poppy seeds on top of the dumpling strips in addition to the salt. Press into the dough with your fingers or a rolling pin. Bake as directed.

Sprinkle Parmesan cheese on top of the dumpling strips. Press into the dough with your fingers or a rolling pin. Bake as directed.

Fried Pastry Strips

Fry whole Anne's Flat Dumpling Strips at 350 degrees in deep fat until brown; drain. Sprinkle with cinnamon-sugar.

You may cut the strips into halves and cut each half into four strips. This will give you eight pieces per strip. Deep-fat-fry until brown; drain. Let cool completely. Put cinnamon-sugar in a sealable bag. Drop the fried pastry strips into the bag. Seal the bag and shake gently to coat.

Strawberry Delight

Use the Fried Pastry Strips (page 95) that have been cut into eight pieces. Arrange six to eight pastry strips on a dessert plate. Top with a big spoonful of sliced and sugared strawberries. Top with six to eight more pastry strips. Spoon whipped cream on the top. Serve immediately.

Serves 1

Boiled Berry Cobbler with Fried Pastry Strips

12 ounces Anne's Flat Dumplings
4 cups water
4 cups mixed berries
1 1/2 cups sugar
1/8 teaspoon cinnamon

Separate a layer of Anne's Flat Dumplings, leaving them on a paper sheet. Cut the dumpling strips into thirds using a pizza cutter. Repeat the process with the remaining dumplings. Combine the water, berries, sugar and cinnamon in a saucepan. Bring to a boil. Drop a few dumpling pieces at a time into the boiling mixture, stirring after each addition. Boil for 8 to 10 minutes or until the dumplings are tender. Cover the saucepan and remove from the heat. The liquid will thicken as it cools and as the dumplings absorb the liquid. Spoon into bowls and top with Fried Pastry Strips.

Serves 6

Family Favorites

NEW
JERSEY
STATE
FAIR

Crispy Cheese Crackers

8 ounces sharp Cheddar cheese, finely shredded
1 cup (2 sticks) butter, softened
2 cups all-purpose flour
1 teaspoon cayenne pepper
1 teaspoon salt
2 cups Rice Crispies cereal

Preheat the oven to 350 degrees. Combine the cheese and butter in a mixing bowl and beat until blended. Combine the flour, cayenne pepper and salt in a bowl. Add to the cheese mixture and mix well. Stir in the cereal. Shape into 1-inch balls and arrange on an ungreased baking sheet. Press with a fork. Bake for 15 minutes or until lightly browned.

Makes 5 dozen

Veggie Bars

2 (8-count) cans refrigerator crescent rolls
16 ounces cream cheese, softened
1 cup mayonnaise
1 envelope Hidden Valley Ranch salad dressing mix
1 cup finely chopped tomatoes
1 cup finely chopped broccoli florets
1 cup finely chopped cauliflower
1 cup (4 ounces) shredded Cheddar cheese

Unroll the crescent roll dough onto a baking sheet, pressing the perforations to seal. Bake as directed on the package; let cool. Combine the cream cheese, mayonnaise and salad dressing mix in a bowl and mix until blended. Spread over the cooled crust. Sprinkle the tomatoes, broccoli and cauliflower over the cream cheese mixture. Sprinkle with the Cheddar cheese. Chill in the refrigerator until serving time.

Serves 10 to 15

Hot Beef Spread

1/2 cup chopped onion
1 tablespoon butter
2 tablespoons dry white wine
8 ounces cream cheese, softened
8 ounces sour cream
1/2 cup mayonnaise
2 1/2 ounces dried beef, finely chopped
1/2 cup pecans, chopped

Preheat the oven to 350 degrees. Sauté the onion in the butter in a skillet until tender. Stir in the wine and simmer for 2 minutes. Add the cream cheese, sour cream, mayonnaise and beef and mix well. Spoon into an 8×8-inch baking dish. Sprinkle with the pecans. Bake for 15 to 20 minutes. Serve with assorted crackers.

Makes 4 cups

Hot Crab Dip

8 ounces cream cheese, softened
1/2 cup mayonnaise
1/4 cup sour cream
2 tablespoons all-purpose flour
1 1/2 teaspoons garlic powder
2 teaspoons Worcestershire sauce
1 tablespoon apple juice
1/4 cup chopped green onions
12 ounces crab meat

Preheat the oven to 350 degrees. Combine the cream cheese, mayonnaise, sour cream, flour, garlic powder and Worcestershire sauce in a bowl and mix well. Add the apple juice, green onions and crab meat and mix gently. Spray a 1-quart baking dish with nonstick cooking spray. Spread the crab meat mixture in the prepared dish. Bake for 30 to 35 minutes or until bubbly and browned. Serve with crackers.

Makes 3 cups

Schoolhouse Rolls

5 cups all-purpose flour	1/4 cup sugar
1 envelope dry yeast	1 1/2 teaspoons salt
1/2 cup mashed potatoes	1 1/2 cups warm water
1/3 cup vegetable oil	(about 100 degrees)

Combine 2 cups of the flour and the yeast in a mixing bowl. Combine the potatoes, oil, sugar, salt and water in a bowl and mix well. Add to the dry ingredients and beat at low speed for 30 seconds, stopping to scrape the side of the bowl frequently. Beat at high speed for 3 minutes. Stir in the remaining 3 cups flour. Chill, covered, for 2 hours or up to 3 days. Punch down the dough and turn out onto a lightly floured surface. Let the dough rest, covered, for 10 minutes. Shape into twenty-four round balls using lightly floured hands. Arrange on a 9×13-inch greased baking sheet. Let rise, covered, for 40 minutes or until doubled in size. Preheat the oven to 400 degrees. Bake for 16 to 20 minutes or until golden brown.

Makes 2 dozen

Banana Nut Bread

3 cups all-purpose flour	3 eggs, beaten
2 cups sugar	1 cup vegetable oil
1 teaspoon baking powder	2 cups mashed ripe bananas
1 teaspoon ground cinnamon	1 (8-ounce) can crushed
3/4 teaspoon salt	pineapple, drained
1 cup chopped pecans	2 teaspoons vanilla extract

Preheat the oven to 350 degrees. Combine the flour, sugar, baking powder, cinnamon and salt in a bowl. Stir in the pecans. Combine the eggs, oil, bananas, pineapple and vanilla in a bowl and mix well. Add to the flour mixture and stir until moistened. Spoon into a greased and floured 4×8-inch loaf pan. Bake for 1 hour and 10 minutes.

Makes 1 loaf

Coffee Cake Muffins

1/4 cup firmly packed light brown sugar
1/4 cup chopped pecans
1 teaspoon ground cinnamon
1 1/2 cups all-purpose flour
1/2 cup granulated sugar
2 teaspoons baking powder
1/4 teaspoon baking soda
1/4 teaspoon salt
1 egg
3/4 cup milk
1/3 cup vegetable oil

Preheat the oven to 400 degrees. Place paper baking cups in a 12-cup muffin pan and spray lightly with nonstick cooking spray. Combine the brown sugar, pecans and cinnamon in a bowl and mix well. Combine the flour, granulated sugar, baking powder, baking soda and salt in a bowl. Make a well in the center of the mixture. Combine the egg, milk and oil and whisk until blended. Add to the flour mixture and stir just until moistened. Spoon 1 tablespoon of the mixture into each muffin cup. Sprinkle with half the brown sugar mixture. Top evenly with the remaining batter. Sprinkle with the remaining brown sugar mixture. Bake for 20 to 24 minutes or until lightly browned.

Serves 12

Ilene's Watergate Salad

12 ounces whipped topping,
1 (6-ounce) package pistachio instant pudding mix
1 (15-ounce) can crushed pineapple, drained
1 (16-ounce) bag miniature marshmallows
1/2 cup sliced almonds or chopped pecans, toasted

Combine the whipped topping and pudding mix in a large bowl and mix well. Stir in the pineapple. Fold in the marshmallows. Spoon into a large serving dish and sprinkle with the almonds. Chill, covered, until serving time.

Serves 6 to 8

Anne's Cucumber-Onion-Tomato Salad

1 onion, thinly sliced
1 cucumber, thinly sliced
2 large tomatoes, cut into wedges
1/2 cup sugar
1/4 cup vinegar
1/2 teaspoon celery seeds
1/4 teaspoon salt

Place the onion, cucumber and tomatoes in a bowl. Combine the sugar, vinegar, celery seeds and salt in a bowl and whisk until blended. Pour over the vegetables. Chill in the refrigerator for 1 hour or longer before serving.

Serves 3 to 4

Corned Beef Hash

3 cups water
2 pounds potatoes, peeled and chopped
1 onion, finely chopped
1 (12-ounce) can corned beef
Salt and pepper to taste

Bring the water to a boil in a heavy saucepan. Add the potatoes and onion and cook until the potatoes are tender. Add the corned beef and stir gently. Cook until the liquid is reduced and the mixture has thickened, stirring occasionally. Season with salt and pepper. May be eaten as is or shaped into patties and browned in a hot skillet.

Serves 6

Hot Dog Chili

2 pounds finely ground beef
1 large onion, finely chopped
1/4 cup tomato paste
1 teaspoon chili powder
Salt and pepper to taste
1/2 cup (or more) water

Cook the ground beef and onion in a skillet until the beef is brown and crumbly, stirring frequently; drain. Add the tomato paste, chili powder, salt and pepper and mix well. Add the water and mix well. Cook for 5 minutes, stirring occasionally and adding additional water to reach the desired consistency.

Serves 36

Salmon Cakes

1 (15-ounce) can salmon
2 eggs
1 sleeve saltine crackers, crushed
1 small onion, finely chopped
Salt and pepper to taste
Vegetable oil for frying

Drain the salmon. Remove the cartilage and skin and flake with a fork. Combine the salmon, eggs, crushed crackers, onion, salt and pepper in a bowl and mix well. Shape into patties. Heat oil in a heavy skillet over medium-high heat. Add the salmon patties and cook until browned on both sides. Remove to a paper towel-lined plate to drain.

Makes 6 to 8 patties

Daddy's Fish Stew

8 ounces bacon
2 to 3 pounds rockfish or flounder,
cut into bite-size portions
2 to 3 pounds white potatoes, peeled and finely chopped
5 to 6 onions, chopped
1 (29-ounce) can tomato sauce
Tabasco sauce to taste
Salt and pepper to taste
1/2 to 1 gallon water
6 to 8 eggs

Fry the bacon in a skillet until brown and crisp; drain, reserving half the drippings. Remove the bacon to a paper towel-lined plate. Combine the fish, potatoes, onions, tomato sauce, Tabasco sauce, salt, pepper, water and the reserved drippings in a large stockpot. Cook over medium heat for 30 minutes or until the fish and potatoes are cooked through, stirring occasionally. Add the eggs one at a time, carefully sliding them into the stockpot so that they don't run. Cook, covered, for 20 minutes. Ladle into soup bowls. Crumble the bacon and sprinkle over the top.

Serves 6 to 8

**This is wonderful on a cold day with fried lacy corn bread.
When I was growing up, Daddy would bring home
rockfish he caught on the Pamlico Ricer and we'd have a feast.**

Collards

3 to 5 pounds collards
$1^1/2$ ham hocks
Salt to taste

Remove and discard the large stems from the collards. Rinse and drain the collards three or four times. Fill a 10- to 12-quart stockpot $^2/3$ full with water. Add the ham hocks and salt and bring to a simmer. Cook for 30 to 45 minutes or until the ham hocks are tender. Remove the meat from the bones and discard the bones. Add the collards to the stockpot. Cook until the collards are tender, stirring occasionally. Drain and chop the collards. Serve with the meat from the ham hocks.

Serves 6 to 8

The time of year will determine how long it takes for the collards to become tender. Check for tenderness by piercing the stem with a fork.

Corn Fritters

2 eggs
1 cup all-purpose flour
1 tablespoon sugar
1 cup fresh, frozen or canned corn
$^1/2$ cup milk
2 tablespoons vegetable oil
Additional vegetable oil for frying

Combine the eggs, flour, sugar, corn, milk and 2 tablespoons oil in a bowl and mix well. Heat enough oil to cover the bottom of a skillet over medium-high heat. Drop the corn mixture by tablespoonfuls into the oil. Cook until browned on both sides, turning once. Remove to a paper towel-lined plate to drain.

Serves 6

Mother's Corn Pudding

1 cup sugar
2 tablespoons all-purpose flour
2 eggs
1 cup milk

1 teaspoon vanilla extract
1 pint fresh, frozen or canned corn
1/4 cup (1/2 stick) butter

Preheat the oven to 325 degrees. Combine the sugar and flour in a bowl. Add the eggs and mix well. Add the milk, vanilla and corn and mix well. Pour into a greased 2-quart baking dish. Dot with the butter. Bake for 45 minutes or until set, stirring every 15 minutes.

Serves 6

Sweet Potato Soufflé

CRUNCH TOPPING
1/2 cup (1 stick) butter, melted
1 cup packed brown sugar
1 cup chopped pecans
1 cup unsweetened grated coconut

SWEET POTATOES
2 pounds sweet potatoes, peeled and cooked until tender

1 1/2 cups sugar
1/2 teaspoon salt
3 eggs
1/2 cup (1 stick) butter, melted
1 (5-ounce) can evaporated milk
1 teaspoon vanilla extract
1/4 teaspoon nutmeg
1/4 teaspoon cinnamon

TOPPING
Combine the butter, brown sugar, pecans and coconut in a bowl and stir until the pecans and coconut are moistened.

SWEET POTATOES
Preheat the oven to 350 degrees. Mash the sweet potatoes in a large bowl. Stir in the sugar, salt, eggs, butter, evaporated milk, vanilla, nutmeg and cinnamon. Spoon into a greased 2-quart baking dish. Spread with the topping. Bake for 30 to 40 minutes.

Serves 8

Stewed Tomatoes

1 onion, finely chopped
¹/₄ cup finely chopped red bell pepper or
yellow bell pepper or a mixture of both
2 (15-ounce) cans diced tomatoes
¹/₄ cup sugar
1 tablespoon cornstarch
2 tablespoons water
Salt and pepper to taste

Sauté the onion and bell pepper in a small amount of water in a deep skillet until the vegetables are tender. Add the tomatoes and sugar and bring to a boil. Combine the cornstarch with 2 tablespoons water in a small bowl and stir until the cornstarch is dissolved. Add to the skillet. Boil until the mixture thickens, stirring constantly. Season with salt and pepper.

Serves 6

I love this spooned over macaroni and cheese for a meatless meal.

Baked Macaroni and Cheese

16 ounces Velveeta cheese, cut into cubes
$^1/_2$ cup (1 stick) butter
1 (5-ounce) can evaporated milk
1 pound elbow macaroni,
cooked and drained
3 eggs, beaten
$^1/_2$ cup (2 ounces) shredded
Cheddar cheese

Preheat the oven to 350 degrees. Combine the Velveeta cheese, butter and evaporated milk in a heavy saucepan. Cook over low heat until the cheese is melted, stirring frequently. Stir in the macaroni. Add the eggs and mix well. Spoon into a baking dish that has been sprayed with nonstick cooking spray. Sprinkle with the Cheddar cheese. Bake for 25 to 35 minutes or until bubbly and browned.

Serves 6

Bobby's Nutty Fingers

1 cup (2 sticks) butter, softened	2 cups all-purpose flour
1/3 cup granulated sugar	1 cup chopped pecans
2 teaspoons water	Confectioners' sugar
2 teaspoons vanilla extract	

Preheat the oven to 325 degrees. Cream the butter and granulated sugar in a mixing bowl. Add the water and vanilla and mix well. Add the flour and pecans and mix well. Shape into balls or "fingers." Arrange on a baking sheet. Bake for 20 minutes. Remove to a wire rack to cool slightly. Roll in confectioners' sugar.

Makes about 3 dozen cookies

Drop Butter Wafers

1/2 cup (1 stick) butter, softened	1 teaspoon vanilla extract
1/2 cup sugar	1 teaspoon grated lemon zest
1 egg	1/2 cup sifted cake flour

Preheat the oven to 375 degrees. Cream the butter and sugar in a mixing bowl. Beat in the egg, vanilla and lemon zest. Add the flour and mix well. Drop by teaspoonfuls onto a cookie sheet. Bake for 7 minutes or until the edges of the cookies are browned. Cool on the cookie sheet for 2 minutes. Remove to a wire rack to cool completely.

Makes 4 dozen cookies

Brown Sugar Cookies

4 cups packed brown sugar
1 cup (2 sticks) butter
4 eggs, beaten
2 cups all-purpose flour
1 teaspoon salt
2 teaspoons baking powder
2 teaspoons vanilla extract
1 1/2 cups chopped pecans
Confectioners' sugar (optional)

Cream the brown sugar and butter in a mixing bowl. Add the eggs and beat until blended. Add the flour, salt and baking powder and mix well. Add the vanilla and beat until blended. Stir in the pecans. Divide the dough into halves and shape each half into a log. Chill, tightly wrapped in plastic wrap, in the refrigerator.

Preheat the oven to 350 degrees. Cut into 1/4-inch slices and arrange on a greased cookie sheet. Bake for 10 to 12 minutes. Remove to a wire rack and sprinkle with confectioners' sugar. Let cool completely. Store in airtight containers.

Makes 4 dozen cookies

Becky's Chewy Bar Cookies

1 (2-layer) package yellow cake mix
1 egg
1/2 cup (1 stick) butter, melted
8 ounces cream cheese, softened
3 eggs
1 (1-pound) package
confectioners' sugar
1 teaspoon lemon juice

Preheat the oven to 350 degrees. Combine the cake mix, 1 egg and the butter in a bowl and mix well. Pat into an ungreased 9×13-inch baking pan. Combine the cream cheese, 3 eggs, the confectioners' sugar and lemon juice in a mixing bowl and beat until blended. Pour over the cake mix layer. At this point, you may sprinkle with coconut or chopped pecans, if desired. Bake for 45 minutes. Let stand until cool and cut into bars.

Makes about 2 dozen bars

Forgotten Cookies

2 egg whites, at room temperature
2/3 cup sugar
1 teaspoon cream of tartar
1 teaspoon vanilla extract
1/2 cup chopped pecans
1 cup (6 ounces) chocolate chips

Preheat the oven to 350 degrees. Cover two large cookie sheets with waxed paper. Beat the egg whites in a mixing bowl until stiff. Add the sugar 1 tablespoon at a time, beating constantly until stiff. Beat in the cream of tartar and vanilla. Add the pecans and chocolate chips and stir gently. Drop by teaspoonfuls onto the cookie sheets. Bake for 2 minutes. Turn off the oven and leave overnight (8 to 10 hours). Do not open the oven door.

Makes 3 dozen cookies

This is an old recipe that I liked when I was young. It was brought to mind when I was looking through my recipe cards. I don't know where it came from, but it was in my mother's handwriting. So easy to make!

Caramels

1 cup (2 sticks) butter
2 1/4 cups firmly packed brown sugar
1 (14-ounce) can sweetened condensed milk
1 cup light corn syrup
1 teaspoon vanilla extract

Line a 9×9-inch pan with foil and butter the foil. Melt 1 cup butter in a heavy 3-quart saucepan over low heat. Add the brown sugar, condensed milk and corn syrup and mix well. Clip a candy thermometer to the side of the pan and increase the heat to medium. Cook to 248 degrees, firm-ball stage. Remove the saucepan from the heat. Stir in the vanilla and quickly pour into the prepared pan. Let stand until firm. Cut into 1-inch squares and wrap each square in plastic wrap or waxed paper.

Makes about 2 3/4 pounds, or 81 (1-inch) squares

Divinity

2 1/2 cups sugar   2 egg whites
1/2 cup light corn syrup   1 teaspoon vanilla extract
1/4 teaspoon salt   1/2 cup chopped pecans (optional)
1/2 cup water

Combine the sugar, corn syrup, salt and water in a heavy saucepan and mix well. Cook over low heat until the sugar dissolves, stirring constantly. Increase the heat to medium and cook to 260 degrees on a candy thermometer, hard-ball stage.

Meanwhile, beat the egg whites in a mixing bowl until stiff peaks form. Add the hot syrup gradually, beating constantly at high speed. Add the vanilla and beat for 4 to 5 minutes or until the mixture is thickened and holds its shape. Stir in the nuts. Drop by teaspoonfuls onto waxed paper. Let stand until cool.

Makes about 40 pieces

Judy's Velveeta Cheese Fudge

1 pound Velveeta cheese, chopped
1 pound (4 sticks) butter
1 cup baking cocoa
4 (1-pound) packages confectioners' sugar, sifted
1 tablespoon vanilla extract
2 cups chopped pecans

Melt the cheese and butter in a saucepan over low heat, stirring occasionally. Combine the baking cocoa and confectioners' sugar in a large bowl. Add the cheese mixture and mix well. Stir in the vanilla and pecans. Pour into a 13×17-inch buttered sheet pan or two 9×9-inch buttered pans and lightly press the mixture all the way to the sides of the pans. Remove the excess oil that rises to the top with a paper towel. Chill in the refrigerator for 15 minutes. Cut into squares. This recipe may be halved or quartered as desired with equally good results.

Makes about 7 pounds

This fudge is excellent for gift giving, as you can make
several varieties using the basic recipe. For parties,
I make at least four varieties by quartering the basic recipe.
This gives my guests a choice and me a beautiful
tray of goodies with so little effort!

Velveeta Cheese Fudge Variations

(Try it; you'll love it!)

PEANUT BUTTER FUDGE

1 pound Velveeta cheese, chopped
1 pound (4 sticks) butter
1 cup peanut butter
4 (1-pound) packages confectioners' sugar, sifted
1 cup chopped roasted peanuts
1 tablespoon vanilla extract

Melt the cheese and butter in a saucepan over low heat, stirring occasionally. Add the peanut butter and mix well. Pour over the confectioners' sugar in a large bowl and mix well. Stir in the peanuts and vanilla. Pour into a buttered 13×17-inch sheet pan or two buttered 9×9-inch pans and complete as directed for the basic fudge recipe (page 118).

PRALINE FUDGE

Substitute 1 cup packed brown sugar for the peanut butter and 2 cups toasted chopped pecans for the roasted peanuts and prepare as directed above.

CONFETTI FUDGE

Omit the peanut butter and substitute ¹/₂ cup chopped red candied cherries, ¹/₂ cup chopped green candied cherries and ¹/₂ cup toasted chopped almonds for the roasted peanuts and prepare as directed above.

Makes about 7 pounds

*Whatever flavors appeal to you may be implemented
in this recipe. I have used coconut, mint, dried cranberries with
orange oil and maple-walnut to name just a few.*

Peanut Butter Balls

1 cup sifted confectioners' sugar
$1/2$ cup creamy peanut butter
3 tablespoons butter, softened
1 pound dipping chocolate

Combine the confectioners' sugar, peanut butter and butter in a bowl and mix well. Shape into 1-inch balls and place on a waxed paper-lined baking sheet. Let stand for 20 minutes or until dry. Melt the chocolate using the package directions. Dip the peanut butter balls in the chocolate and return to the baking sheet. Let stand until dry. Store, tightly covered, in a cool dry location.

Makes about 30 pieces

Double Peanut Clusters

1 cup (6 ounces) semisweet chocolate chips
$1/2$ cup creamy peanut butter
$1^1/2$ cups roasted peanuts

Combine the chocolate and peanut butter in a microwave-safe bowl. Microwave for 1 minute. Stir to see if the mixture is melted. Microwave until melted, stirring every few seconds. Add the peanuts and mix well. Drop by heaping teaspoonfuls onto waxed paper. Let cool completely. Store in an airtight container in the refrigerator.

Makes about 30

Pralines

¾ cup granulated sugar
¾ cup packed light brown sugar
1 (5-ounce) can evaporated milk
½ cup (1 stick) butter, softened
½ cup coarsely chopped pecans
1 teaspoon vanilla extract

Butter a 12×15-inch piece of foil and set aside. Combine the granulated sugar, brown sugar and evaporated milk in a heavy 8 inch skillet. Bring to a boil and boil until the sugar is dissolved, stirring constantly. Check for soft-ball stage, 234 to 240 degrees on a candy thermometer, after about 3 to 5 minutes. Remove the pan from the heat once soft-ball stage is reached. Add the butter; do not stir. Do not stir. Sprinkle with the pecans and pour in the vanilla; do not stir. Let the mixture cool for 20 minutes. Beat vigorously using a wooden spoon until the mixture thickens and loses its luster. Drop by tablespoonfuls onto the prepared foil. Let stand until set. This may also be poured into a buttered 8×8-inch pan and cut into squares.

Makes about 2 dozen pralines

***This recipe was given to my husband in 1963
by a fellow airman when we were stationed at Biloxi AFB, about
sixty miles from New Orleans.***

Microwave Peanut Brittle

1 cup raw peanuts
1 cup sugar
1/2 cup light corn syrup
1/8 teaspoon salt
1 teaspoon butter
1 teaspoon vanilla extract
1 teaspoon baking soda

Combine the peanuts, sugar, corn syrup and salt in a 1-quart microwave-safe bowl with a handle and mix well. Microwave on High for 8 minutes, stirring halfway through the cooking time. Stir in the butter and vanilla. Microwave on High for 2 minutes. Add the baking soda and stir quickly until the mixture is light and foamy. Pour onto a lightly greased baking sheet immediately, spreading thinly. Let stand until set. Break into pieces and store in a tightly sealed container.

Makes 1 pound

Anne's Vanilla Wafer Cake

2 cups sugar
1 cup (2 sticks) butter, softened
6 eggs
1/2 cup milk
1 (12-ounce) package vanilla wafers, crushed
1 cup flaked coconut
1 cup chopped pecans

Preheat the oven to 325 degrees. Cream the sugar and butter in a mixing bowl until fluffy. Add the eggs one at a time, beating well after each addition. Add the milk and crushed cookies and mix well. Fold in the coconut and pecans. Pour into a greased and floured bundt pan. Bake for 1 hour or until the cake tests done.

Serves 16

1-2-3-4 Cake

1 cup (2 sticks) butter, softened
2 cups sugar
4 eggs
3 cups sifted self-rising flour
1 cup milk
1 teaspoon vanilla extract

Preheat the oven to 350 degrees. Cream the butter and sugar in a mixing bowl until light and fluffy. Add the eggs one at a time, beating well after each addition. Add the flour to the creamed mixture alternately with the milk, mixing well after each addition. Stir in the vanilla. Pour into three waxed paper-lined 9-inch cake pans. Bake for 25 minutes.

Makes 3 (9-inch) cake layers

Mother's Exquisite Coconut Cake

3 (9-inch) cake layers from
1-2-3-4 Cake recipe (page 108)

COCONUT FILLING
2 cups sugar
1 cup half-and-half or whole milk
3 tablespoons light corn syrup
1 teaspoon vanilla extract
3 cups grated fresh or frozen coconut

ITALIAN MERINGUE ICING
(SIMILAR TO SEVEN-MINUTE ICING)
1 cup sugar
6 tablespoons water
6 egg whites
1/4 teaspoon cream of tartar
6 tablespoons sugar
1 teaspoon vanilla extract
1/2 cup grated fresh or frozen coconut

FILLING

Combine the sugar, half-and-half and corn syrup in a heavy saucepan over medium heat and mix well. Stir in the vanilla and coconut. Cook until the mixture thickens, stirring constantly. Spread between the layers and over the top of the cake.

ICING

Combine 1 cup sugar and the water in a small saucepan and bring to a boil; reduce the heat. Cook to 245 degrees on a candy thermometer, stirring frequently. Beat the egg whites and cream of tartar in a metal bowl until medium peaks form. Add 6 tablespoons sugar and beat until medium peaks form. Add the sugar mixture gradually, beating constantly. Add the vanilla. Beat until medium peaks form and mixture is of the desired spreading consistency. Spread over the top and side of the cake. Sprinkle with the coconut, pressing lightly into the icing.

Serves 12

You may use packaged flaked coconut if desired. Place the coconut in a blender and pulse until finely grated.

Coconut Pineapple Cake

3 (9-inch) cake layers from
1-2-3-4 Cake recipe (page 124)

PINEAPPLE FILLING
2 cups sugar
1/4 cup cornstarch
1 cup crushed pineapple
1 cup water

CREAM CHEESE FROSTING
1/2 cup (1 stick) butter, softened
3 ounces cream cheese, softened
1 (1-pound) package confectioners' sugar
1/4 cup pineapple juice
1 teaspoon vanilla extract
6 ounces frozen coconut, thawed

FILLING

Combine the sugar and cornstarch in a heavy saucepan over low heat. Drain the pineapple, reserving the juice for the frosting. Add the pineapple and water to the sugar mixture. Cook over low heat until the mixture thickens, stirring constantly . Remove from the heat and let stand until cool. Spread between the layers and over the top of the cake.

FROSTING

Beat the butter and cream cheese in a mixing bowl until fluffy. Add the confectioners' sugar, pineapple juice and vanilla gradually, beating constantly. Spread over the side of the cake. Sprinkle with the coconut, pressing lightly into the frosting.

Serves 12

Grandma Briley's
Orange Cake with Meringue

3 (9-inch) cake layers from 1-2-3-4 Cake recipe (page 124)

ORANGE FILLING
1 1/2 cups sugar
5 1/2 tablespoons all-purpose flour
1/2 teaspoon salt
1 1/2 cups fresh orange juice
2 tablespoons lemon juice
1/4 cup (1/2 stick) butter
3 egg yolks, beaten
3 tablespoons grated orange zest

MERINGUE
3 egg whites
3/4 cup sugar
1/4 teaspoon cream of tartar

FILLING
Combine the sugar, flour, salt, orange juice, lemon juice, butter, egg yolks and orange zest in a saucepan and cook over medium heat until thickened, stirring constantly. Chill in the refrigerator. Place the cake on an ovenproof cake plate. Spread the filling between the layers of the cake.

MERINGUE
Combine the egg whites, sugar and cream of tartar in a mixing bowl and beat until stiff peaks form. Spread over the top and side of the cake. Bake at 350 degrees until the meringue browns. Let stand until cool. Chill in the refrigerator until serving time.

Serves 12

Becky's Chocolate Chess Pie

2 unbaked (9-inch) pie shells
3 eggs
$1^7/8$ cups sugar
$1/2$ cup (1 stick) butter, softened
$1/2$ cup baking cocoa
$1^1/2$ teaspoons vanilla extract
1 (5-ounce) can evaporated milk
$1^1/2$ teaspoons whole milk

Preheat the oven to 425 degrees. Prick the bottoms and sides of the pie shells several times with a fork. Bake for 4 to 5 minutes. Reduce the oven temperature to 350 degrees. Combine the eggs, sugar, butter, baking cocoa and vanilla in a mixing bowl and beat until blended. Add the evaporated milk and whole milk and mix well by hand. Pour into the prepared pie shells and bake for 35 minutes.

Serves 12 to 16

My sister, Becky (November 17, 1948–June 29, 2006),
the youngest of my siblings, loved to cook, and she was well known
for her desserts, especially her chocolate pies. She could whip
up a batch and be down the road with them before they got cold;
that is, if the fish weren't biting by her pier.

Anne's Chocolate Meringue Pie

3/4 cup sugar
2 tablespoons cornstarch
2 cups milk
2 ounces unsweetened chocolate
3 egg yolks
2 tablespoons butter or margarine, softened
1 baked (9-inch) pie shell
3 egg whites
1/2 teaspoon cream of tartar
6 tablespoons sugar

Combine 3/4 cup sugar and the cornstarch in a microwave-safe bowl. Stir in the milk. Add the chocolate. Microwave on High for 6 to 8 minutes or until smooth and thick, stirring after 3 minutes. Stir a small amount of the mixture into the egg yolks in a bowl. Pour the egg yolk mixture into the chocolate mixture and mix well. Microwave on Medium-High for 3 minutes, stirring once. Add the butter and stir until melted. Pour into the pie shell.

Preheat the oven to 425 degrees. Beat the egg whites and cream of tartar in a mixing bowl until foamy. Beat in 6 tablespoons sugar 1 tablespoon at a time. Beat until stiff and glossy. Spoon over the chocolate filling, carefully sealing to the edge of the pie shell. Bake for 8 to 10 minutes or until the meringue is browned.

Serves 6 to 8

Peggy's Orange Icebox Pie

1 small package orange gelatin	Grated zest of 1 orange
1 cup hot water	1 (12-ounce) can evaporated milk
1 cup sugar	Finely ground vanilla wafers
Juice of 1 orange	

Combine the gelatin and water in a bowl and stir until the gelatin is dissolved. Add the sugar, orange juice and orange zest and mix well. Chill just until beginning to set. Beat the evaporated milk in a bowl until foamy. Fold into the gelatin mixture. Sprinkle ground vanilla wafers over the bottom of a 9×9-inch dish. Pour in the gelatin mixture. Sprinkle with additional ground vanilla wafers. Chill until serving time.

Serves 6

David's Sweet Potato Pie

1 pound sweet potatoes, cooked, peeled and mashed	Nutmeg to taste
2 eggs	Cinnamon to taste
1/2 cup sugar	Allspice to taste
1 1/2 cups evaporated milk	Vanilla extract
2 tablespoons butter	2 partially baked (9-inch) pie shells

Preheat the oven to 350 degrees. Combine the sweet potatoes, eggs, sugar, evaporated milk, butter, nutmeg, cinnamon, allspice and vanilla in a mixing bowl and beat until blended. Pour into the pie shells. Bake for 45 to 50 minutes or until set.

Serves 12 to 16

Pecan Pie

1 1/2 cups pecans, chopped
2 unbaked (9-inch) pie shells
3 eggs
1 2/3 cups packed brown sugar
1/2 cup (1 stick) butter, melted
Dash of salt
1 teaspoon vanilla extract
1 teaspoon vinegar

Preheat the oven to 350 degrees. Sprinkle the pecans evenly over the bottoms of the pie shells. Beat the eggs in a mixing bowl. Add the brown sugar, butter, salt, vanilla and vinegar and mix well. Pour over the pecans. Place the filled pie shells on a baking sheet. Bake for 35 minutes.

Serves 12 to 16

To make Chess Pies, prepare the pies as directed above, omitting the pecans. To make Coconut Pies, prepare the pies as directed above, omitting the pecans and adding 1 1/2 cups coconut.

Basic Meringue

3 egg whites, at room temperature
1/2 teaspoon vanilla extract
1/4 teaspoon cream of tartar
6 tablespoons sugar

Combine the egg whites, vanilla and cream of tartar in a glass or metal mixing bowl and beat until foamy. Add the sugar 1 tablespoon at a time, beating constantly. Beat until the sugar is dissolved and stiff peaks form. Spread over hot pie filling of your choice, spreading to the edge of the piecrust to prevent shrinkage. Bake as directed for the pie recipe.

Makes enough meringue to top 1 pie

Meringue seems to give many cooks problems. Be sure the egg whites are at room temperature and that the bowl and beaters are grease-free. The cream of tartar helps to stabilize the mixture. When beating, look for gloss, sharp peaks, and small, almost invisible, air pockets. Seal your meringue to the edge of your pie so that it doesn't shrink. Cut through the meringue with a wet knife.

Meringue can be dressed up by adding fruit slices, toasted coconut, or chocolate shavings once the pie has cooled.

Pecan Tart

1 (1-crust) pie pastry
$^1/_2$ cup (1 stick) butter
$^1/_4$ cup honey
$^1/_2$ cup packed brown sugar
$^1/_4$ cup granulated sugar
2 cups chopped pecans
$^1/_4$ cup evaporated milk
1 teaspoon vanilla extract
$^1/_4$ cup semisweet chocolate chips

Preheat the oven to 325 degrees. Unfold the pastry into a 9-inch tart pan. Fit the pastry into the pan and trim the edge. Prick the side and bottom of the pastry several times using a fork. Bake for 12 minutes. Maintain the oven temperature.

Combine the butter, honey, brown sugar and granulated sugar in a heavy skillet and bring to a boil. Boil for 3 minutes, stirring frequently. Remove from the heat. Add the pecans, evaporated milk and vanilla and mix well. Pour into the prepared tart shell and bake for 15 to 20 minutes. Let cool for 30 minutes.

Microwave the chocolate chips in a microwave-safe bowl for 30 seconds or until melted. Drizzle the chocolate over the cooled tart. Remove the bottom from the tart pan and place the tart on a 10-inch platter. Cut into wedges to serve.

Serves 6 to 8

Mother's Chocolate Biscuit Pudding

8 to 10 biscuits	1 cup milk
1 1/2 cups sugar	4 eggs, beaten
1/2 cup baking cocoa	1 teaspoon vanilla extract
3 tablespoons butter	

Preheat the oven to 350 degrees. Crumble the biscuits into a bowl. Combine the sugar, baking cocoa, butter and milk in a heavy saucepan. Cook until the sugar and baking cocoa are dissolved, stirring frequently. Add the eggs one at a time, stirring after each addition. Stir in the vanilla. Pour over the crumbled biscuits and stir gently. Spoon into a greased 9×13-inch baking pan. Bake for 30 to 35 minutes. Serve warm with a little sweetened condensed milk drizzled over the top or with a scoop of ice cream.

Serves 6

Pootabear's Pineapple Stuffing

1/2 cup (1 stick) butter, softened	1 (15-ounce) can crushed
1 1/2 cups sugar	pineapple, drained
5 eggs	3 cups your favorite cubed bread
	(I like Italian sweet bread)

Preheat the oven to 350 degrees. Cream the butter, sugar and eggs in a mixing bowl until fluffy. Add the pineapple and bread cubes and stir gently. Spoon into a greased square 1 1/2-quart baking dish. Bake for 30 minutes or until the desired degree of brownness is reached. Serve warm, with a drizzle of sweetened condensed milk. It is also delicious cold.

Serves 6

Grandma Taylor's Peach Pandowdy

6 cups thickly sliced fresh or canned peaches
1 tablespoon lemon juice
1/2 cup sugar
1 tablespoon cornstarch
1 cup all-purpose flour
2 tablespoons sugar
1/4 teaspoon salt
1 tablespoon butter
1/2 cup heavy cream

Preheat the oven to 375 degrees. Place the peaches in a medium bowl. Sprinkle with the lemon juice. Combine 1/2 cup sugar and the cornstarch in a bowl. Sprinkle over the peaches and stir gently to coat. Spoon into a 2- to 2 1/2-quart baking dish.

Combine the flour, 2 tablespoons sugar and the salt in a bowl. Cut in the butter using a pastry blender until the mixture resembles fine crumbs. Make a well in the center and pour in the cream. Stir with a fork until the dough pulls away from the side of the bowl. Roll the dough on a floured surface until it is big enough to cover the baking dish. Cut a 2-inch cross in the center of the dough. Place over the peaches, tucking in around the side. Turn back one corner of the cut dough to reveal the filling. Bake for 45 minutes or until bubbly and golden brown.

Serves 8

Bread
for the
Journey

String of Pearls
Pat James

As I was preparing this introduction, the Holy Spirit reminded me of a beautiful cultured pearl necklace I received from my parents when I graduated from high school. He spoke to me that it was a prophetic gesture of the spiritual string of pearls I would receive some forty years later from Him. It appears my destiny was to impart to you some of what I have learned over the years walking with the Lord.

In 2002, the Lord encouraged me to make a list of these pearls and string them together to form a graceful devotional necklace. Proverbs 1:9 encourages us that wisdom should be "a garland to grace your head and a chain to adorn your neck." Following each pearl are scripture references for your extended study. Some selections are short and to the point, while others have illustrations from my own life. May this string of devotional pearls provide you with the grace, understanding, and wisdom needed to experience the blessings of God as you fulfill your destiny in the kingdom of God.

The "word of wisdom" mentioned in 1 Corinthians 12:8 is one of God's spiritual gifts to believers. Whenever the Holy Spirit has graciously released this gift through me for the benefit of others, I have experienced the anointing of the Holy Spirit and the person who received them was blessed with understanding and encouragement. The thoughts that follow are pearls of wisdom the Lord has given to me over a number of years. They come out of countless hours of meditating on the Word and listening to the Holy Spirit who has been my faithful teacher and counselor.

Old and new believers alike may have a tremendous zeal for serving God and a consuming passion to reform the church, but one thing they often lack is wisdom. We are not born again with the wisdom that comes from our Heavenly Father above. Acquiring true godly wisdom requires years of walking in the Spirit and learning many lessons—some the hard way. I hope the following pearls will supply you with more understanding and grace needed to serve the people of God and the spiritual discernment to understand the ways of God. Now after a lifetime of following after God, growing in Christ, and the knowledge of the Holy Spirit, this is my gift to you—fifty-five pearls of wisdom to help God's children be overcomers in this life.

May you be richly blessed with God's presence and anointing as you read these pearls of wisdom.

Pat James
Tree of Life Ministries
Easter 2004

Addendum—On December 25, 2005, my daughter Mary and her fiancé Kent Tinsley gave me a lovely pearl cross for Christmas. The card enclosed with the cross informed me that pearls represented wisdom in Christian art. That evening, the Holy Spirit prompted me to retrieve this long-neglected collection of pearls from the deep recesses of my computer. He gently chided me with, "It is not doing anyone any good in your computer. Print it as it is and give it away." So in obedience to the Spirit, here it is—without any editing or changes.

1.

Have you wondered why you are not growing in Christ-likeness as you know you should
be? Perhaps the reason is you have not submitted to the dealings of the Holy Spirit for the crucifixion
of your flesh. You are continuing to live life in the flesh by your own power and understanding. You are
continuing to demand your rights and desires before those of others. One must volunteer to be
crucified before change can happen. Seeds that fall upon the ground and don't get buried become food
for the animals. Except a seed fall into the ground and die, it cannot spring forth to resurrection life. We
are the seed that has to be buried and reckoned dead before Christ can be made alive in us.

John 12:24

2.

The spouse God gives to us is just the person we need in our life to help us be conformed
into the image of Jesus Christ. They were given to us by God to help us die to our sinful nature, and
experience resurrection life. If your spouse is the opposite of you, it is not by accident, but
by divine purpose. A gemologist uses a rock tumbler to transform unsightly, rough pieces of gravel
into beautiful semi-precious stones. When given enough time, water and grit, they are polished
into beautiful gems that have much more value and beauty than the original.

Romans 8:29

3.

We can fall on the Rock of Jesus Christ, or the rock will fall on us. It is our choice. Our Heavenly Father gives us free will to make decisions. If we study His Word and follow the leading of the Holy Spirit, we will make Christ-like choices in life. We must choose to trust and obey the scriptures even when we don't fully understand. Rocks represent hard places in our life when things do not go like we think they should. We can choose to obey God's Word and give a godly response, or we can refuse. If we choose to do it God's way, we will be blessed. If we choose to have our own way, God will need to chastise and correct us. Circumstances and people will be more difficult than before, because we have not learned the way of righteousness.

I Peter 2:4-8

4.

Conflict is an opportunity to die to self and live to be more like Jesus. Conflict produces change. As long as there is no conflict, change does not take place. People continue along in the same manner, content to stay the same. One day I noticed a large tree growing beside the sidewalk in my neighborhood. The roots had pushed the concrete up and broken it into pieces. The concrete would have been content to stay in one piece undisturbed, but the oak tree needed room to grow. Something had to give. How much better when we yield to the desires and needs of others do they have room to grow.

Romans 12:1

5.

It is true that opposites attract. We instinctively see in each other what we are missing in ourselves. A magnet has two opposite poles that attract or repel iron or steel objects. When the object is placed near one pole, it is drawn to it or repelled by it. For the most part, we are attracted to other's strengths and repelled by their weaknesses. We are magnetically drawn to people who will balance our personality. Two people with the same weakness will only pull each other down or lead each other astray. So God puts opposites together for balance and stability. Parents who are opposites provide balanced perspectives, emotional support, spiritual insight, and safety for their children.

Matthew 15:14

6.

As the old saying goes, "It takes one to know one." Before you criticize someone of a fault, stop to ask the Holy Spirit if you are guilty of doing the same thing. You might be surprised by the answer. I have discovered over the years that people tend to point out the same faults in others that they are blind to in themselves. That's how you unconsciously recognize it so well. You are guilty of the same sin, but have been blinded by self-deception and denial. People who complain that others are critical and judgmental, usually have the same stronghold operating in themselves. And that's the simple truth.

Matthew 7:1-9

7.

Healthy relationships are built on respect for one another. It is the foundation for all other attitudes. Without respect, there can not be positive relationships. If respect is gone, love will be impossible to maintain. Guard your heart and be careful to maintain respect for others, even if they don't show respect toward you. Husbands are instructed to love their wives, however wives are told to respect their husbands. They need to show respect even when they are not loved or appreciated by their spouses. Also, do not tolerate disrespect from others for your loved ones. Disrespect undermines love, understanding, and commitment.

Ephesians 5:33

8.

The secret of working through adversity is maintaining a grateful heart. Your situation could be a lot worse except for the grace God has extended to you. Gratefulness assures one of a positive attitude when the circumstances dictate hard times and negative outcomes. When I am tempted to complain of my own circumstances, I do not have to look far to find others with far worse problems than I have. "There I go, but for the grace of God," was instilled in me by my mother.

As a child, we often went to the Home for the Crippled in Memphis, Tennessee, to provide holiday programs, sing Christmas carols, or give birthday gifts. Seeing others with Multiple Sclerosis, birth defects, or amputations living on stretchers or in wheelchairs for the rest of their lives really impacted my young spirit. Gratefulness will carry you through any adversity. Be grateful you are alive with a strong body and mind. Be grateful you have loved ones who support you. Be grateful that God will be with you and never forsake you.

Colossians 3:15-17

9.

Practice the spiritual law of sowing and reaping to get the victory over difficult situations. Christ in us can sow seeds of the fruit of the Spirit, which will come back to us multiplied.

One year I was substituting for three months in the fourth grade for a teacher out on maternity leave. It was one of the most difficult challenges I have ever experienced. Daily I found myself frustrated with the students' anger, disrespect, and rude behavior. I found myself becoming like them: mad, yelling, and on the verge of tears. I had to maintain control of the classroom and get the victory over this stressful situation. I wanted to lay down the law and demand that they adhere to the school of rules, or suffer the consequences. After all, children need to obey the rules, right?

However, the Holy Spirit instructed me to sow the fruit of the Spirit into my students instead of focusing on their sinfulness. I began sowing seeds of love, joy, peace, patience, kindness, goodness, and self-control. Daily prayer on the way to school enabled me to demonstrate these Christ-like attributes toward my students even when I didn't feel like it. I began greeting them in the morning with hugs, compliments, and encouraging comments. I patiently listened to their problems, maintained my peace, and demonstrated self-control. Before long there was an amazing change in several of the worst students. They began to respond with admiration and respect toward me. They recognized that Christ in me genuinely loved and cared for them, and I began to reap good fruit in return from them.

Galatians 5:22-26, 6:7-10; II Corinthians 3:6.

10.

When God calls you to do something, he will supply all the money, materials, and people to help you do it. Our responsibility is to obey in faith, believing He is directing our steps as we go. Noah was commanded by God to build an ark and then fill it with animals and food. It took him one hundred years to accomplish that task, during which he faced ridicule from family, friends, and neighbors. They had never even heard of rain, nor seen a boat. Noah trusted God to supply everything he needed and never questioned how it would get done. He believed God was a man of his word, and what He said, He would do. If rain was coming upon the earth, flooding every living thing, then Noah wanted to be ready. Our responsibility is to make sure we have heard from God and have our orders clearly defined. The rest is up to Him.

Genesis 6-8

11.

From time to time, even God needs a reminder. That's why he placed the rainbow in the clouds. It serves as a reminder to him of his everlasting covenant with all living creatures to bless them and never again to destroy all life on earth with a flood. God is a covenant-keeping God, and life will go well with us if we maintain our covenant relationship with Him. That means we are to love Him and obey His word. The rainbow is the first of many covenants God made with his people. His desire is to establish a loving relationship that will last a thousand generations. If we will be faithful to Him, He will remain faithful to us. The next time you witness a rainbow in the stormy sky, give thanks to God for his faithfulness to you.

Genesis 9:12-17

12.

Our adversary will take us to court even if we are only 10 percent wrong. If we refuse to repent, blame others, or justify our actions and attitudes, then we will find ourselves in prison until there is complete restitution. Does it not seem strange that our adversary knows when we are wrong and takes full advantage of it? You see, God created "the adversary" to test us and refine us as pure gold. All the dross has to be refined out of us, even that last little bit of sinful nature that would keep us separated from God. As long as we maintain our own self-righteousness, or are determined to have our own way, we will find ourselves in a prison of our own making. And we will not get out until we have paid the last penny.

Matthew 5:25-26

13.

Unity brings about power and accomplishment even for the wrong motives. The story of the Tower of Babel illustrates the corporate pride of man—unity for the wrong reason. The whole world had one language and a common speech. There on the plains of Shinar, men decided to build a tower that would reach to heaven so that they could make a name for themselves, a flagrant violation of God's command to "fill the earth." "Nothing they planned to do will be impossible for them." The Lord came down and confused their language so they couldn't understand each other. God, Satan, and the disciple Paul understood the power of confusion. Confusion divides and destroys a work.

Genesis 11; Matthew 12:22-28; Acts 23:6-10

14.

Without the fear of God in us, we will not obey Him. Our obedience to God's Word is proof that we have an awesome, reverent respect for His power and authority. Fearing God means we honor, worship, trust, and serve Him as the one true God. Disobedience is evidence of our unbelief. Much of the world today does not know God nor fear His power. That is why sin is so rampant. It is the responsibility of each generation to pass along the miraculous stories of how God has been their provider and protector. When one generation fails to do this, the next one does not have a healthy respect for God. Doubt and unbelief take hold of their minds and they begin to openly disobey God's Word without any understanding of the disastrous consequences. The Lord delights in those who fear Him, in those who put their trust in His unfailing love.

Psalms 145:4, 147:11; Proverbs 9:10-12

15.

Give us this day our daily bread. Some seasons, God's provision may come only in daily amounts in order to test our trust in Him to provide for each new day. Storing up provisions for tomorrow can mean we are anxious and not trusting God. He is testing our obedience, and we are given the opportunity to prove our trust in Him.

Exodus 16; Matthew 6:11

16.

God tests His children in order to prove what is in their heart. Obedience, trust, and faith have to be proven first before God can bless us. Only then can He bring us into our destiny and purpose for living. He already knows what is in our hearts, but do we?

In 1980, we sold everything we had and moved to Pensacola, Florida, to attend Liberty Bible School. After six months, we were out of money and Tommy still did not have a good job. Had we missed God? Surely if we had heard correctly, God would have provided for us. As time went on, anxiety, fear, and even resentment arose from our hearts, but still not relief.

Finally, God spoke to us that we were experiencing a test to see if we were really going to serve Him whatever the cost. This experience was quite humbling and not one we enjoyed. When we answered, "Yes, Lord," the door was opened to a marvelous job which blessed us financially for years to come. God often gives the test first and then reveals the lesson that was learned. I called this experience "From Food Stamps to Lake Charlene."

See Genesis 22 for the story of how God tested Abraham.

17.

Jesus would never have made it through His experience on the Cross if He had focused on His pain, suffering, and humiliation. Instead, He focused on the joy set before Him scorning its shame. He was looking forward to overcoming Satan and sitting down at the right hand of God. Shame will come to us in many ways throughout our lives. We have the choice to embrace it as a part of who we are, or reject it as a lie from the enemy. Shame says we are inferior, a failure, rejected, or unloved. The Word says…we are accepted and loved by God, successful through Christ, and empowered by the Holy Spirit.

Hebrews 12:2

18.

Objective seeing and hearing are prerequisites for understanding. The Holy Spirit gives revelation of spiritual truths as we take time to look and to listen with an open heart. Our own biases and limited experience can deceive us and make us think we have heard from God when indeed we have not. Neutral thinking is the key to hearing what the Spirit has to say. Centuries ago, man used to think the world was flat and you could sail off the edge of it. Time, experience, and knowledge have changed our beliefs. Now we know how to fly off into space and return safely. Be careful not to let your own limited experience in spiritual matters set the perimeters of your beliefs. Be open-minded and allow the Spirit of God to guide your understanding.

Matthew 13:11-23

19.

The real you...is Christ in you. When Satan tells you that you are rotten to the core, remind him that you have been born again and your old, carnal nature is now dead and buried. You are a new creation, growing daily in Christ. He is living his life through you. The old you was rotten to the core, but the new you is being re-created in the image and likeness of Jesus Christ.

Romans 6; John 3:3-8

20.

Sometimes we have to wrestle with God until He blesses us. Overcomers struggle with God and with men in the spirit realm until the victory is achieved. Both Jacob and Jesus wrestled in prayer during the night hours for God's power and grace to be manifested the next day. Disaster may be averted, or we may be given the strength to go through the adversity. Either way, we are trusting in God's divine intervention.

Genesis 32:22-32; Matthew 26:36-46

21.

The fear of God in us produces abundant blessing on us: prosperity, provision, protection, success, wisdom, strength, a good life, health, and godly families. Not to mention miracles and eternal life. It is imperative that we teach our children to fear God and love and obey Him. Without this awesome respect for God, disobedience takes hold of the next generation and there is a great falling away.

Exodus 1:17-21; Deuteronomy 6:13-25; Psalms 36:1-4, 111:10; Proverbs 9:10, 19:23

22.

Circumcision and Passover are to the Christian faith, as conception and birth are to all of nature. One must first enter into a covenant agreement to love and obey God before he can appropriate the blood of Christ for the atonement of sin and divine protection over his life. As in nature, first comes commitment, and then comes provision. Conception occurs when two agree to mate and the birth of their offspring follows. In the Old Testament, circumcision is to Passover, as repentance is to the blood of Christ in the New Testament. "Blessed is he whose transgressions are forgiven, whose sins are covered."

Exodus 12:43–51; Psalms 32; Acts 3:19

23.

Our children were the seed in our loins when we made our commitment to Christ. When we repent and are born again into the kingdom of God, then our children and grandchildren are heirs to the same covenant with God that we enjoy. If we are called by God, then they are called by God as well. Both Satan and our heirs need to be reminded of this from time to time. We are not our own, but bought and paid for by the blood of Christ at the Cross of Calvary.

Acts 3:25; Galatians 3:26–4:7

24.

Grumbling and complaining bring on a meager existence. They show our lack of trust in God and anxiety about our future provision. When the Israelites grumbled against God, He responded with manna and quail for them. Most people marvel at God's divine provision for His children, but the reality is for forty years there was no variety, and only limited provision. If we want God's blessing of abundance, we must demonstrate gratefulness, thanksgiving, and trust.

Exodus 16

25.

Worship is to winning, as fuel is to a fire. A fire needs fuel to burn and without it will go out. When the enemy attacks us, our best strategy may be to worship our Abba Father. For He gives victory over our enemies. This tactic demonstrates our faith and trust in Him. Worship brings Him honor and glory and gives us the strength to fight the battle. Worship provides the fuel we need to fight the battle of faith. "The Lord is my banner."

Exodus 16

26.

Does your illness have a spiritual root? When the Israelites contracted an infectious skin disease, they were isolated from others and sent outside the camp. The priest sacrificed sin offerings to the Lord to atone for their sin. The blood of a dove, three lambs, and a log of oil were sprinkled on the person. When the sin was atoned for, the person was pronounced clean. Disease was associated with sin in their lives and good health was a sign of righteous living. Sometimes the sickness we contract is due to sin in our lives or that of our ancestors. David's bones wasted away and his strength was sapped when he refused to acknowledge his sin before God. When he repented and asked forgiveness, he was healed of his affliction. Ask the Holy Spirit to show you what you need to repent of and ask forgiveness for so you can apply the blood of Jesus to your body for healing.

Isaiah 53; Psalms 32:1-5, 103:1-5

27.

Priming the pump produces results. If you have ever lived in the country and had to get your water from a well, you know firsthand what happens when the electricity goes out. Without electricity, the pump loses its pressure. To get the water flowing again, first you have to pour water in the pump to create the vacuum needed. The same is true with life in the Spirit. You have to receive Christ first, before you can draw out the living water of Jesus Christ. Just like the analogy of the well, there has to be that divine connection of Spirit to spirit before life can flow out of us.

John 4:13

28.

The external work of the Holy Spirit is to give our minds the divine revelation of Jesus Christ's atonement for our sin. To have more and deeper revelations, you must invite the Spirit of God to dwell within you. He works internally to quicken our spirit, counsel us, comfort us, and guide us into truth. For centuries, man has tried to understand God apart from revelation by the Holy Spirit. It simply can't be done. It takes the Holy Spirit working from within to open the eyes of your spiritual understanding.

John 14:26

29.

Self-righteous judgment and condemnation of God's leaders can make you susceptible to physical disease and pain. Miriam's attitude and criticism of Moses prompted God to strike her with leprosy. She was not afraid to criticize God's servant, and He dealt with her severely. Bitterness and resentment can be precursors of arthritis, stroke, and heart disease.

Numbers 12

30.

Like Jesus, we should practice the law of multiplication. He took the little that he had, gave thanks, broke it, and passed it out to others. Seven loaves of bread and a few small fish fed four thousand one day. As ministers of God and members of the family of God, we should exercise the gifts the spirit gives to us and impart blessing to others. In so doing, the blessing is multiplied to thousands beyond ourselves. Giving thanks before God acknowledges our dependency on Him and shows our faith in His ability to meet our needs.

Mark 8

31.

Faith and fear are the two most important attitudes in a person's life. Faith brings us into God's blessings and fear of God keeps us from disobedience. Satan tries to rob us of faith and give us a spirit of fear instead. It's the "what ifs" that cause anxiety. Where do we put our faith? Whom do we fear the most?

Psalms 34; Philippians 4:6

32.

God gives us abundant life, but we can lose it. Obedience and trusting in God produces blessings in our lives: provision, protection, and prosperity. Disobedience and not trusting in Him produces curses: death, destruction, and destitution.

Deuteronomy 28:11

33.

What do Balaam, a man who practiced occult divination, and Jesus, the son of God, have in common? They both understood how important it was to speak only the words God gave to them to speak. Likewise, we are instructed to speak the words the Holy Spirit gives to us. Believe that the Spirit of the Father wants to speak to others through us.

Numbers 22; Matthew 10:20

34.

Objects of God's wrath are prepared for destruction. Objects of His mercy are prepared for glory. God raised up Pharaoh to be a hard-hearted and stubborn man and put him in charge of ruling over Egypt. God demonstrated His sovereign power and purpose in his election. He does this in order to make known the riches of His glory toward His people whom He also has prepared in advance to receive His glory. Yet, God also gives us the free will to choose our eternal destiny.

Exodus 4-15; Joshua 6:21

35.

Patience is a virtue that allows us to experience God's perfect timing. He alone can bring together the people, the resources, and the provision necessary to produce His perfect plan for our lives. Sarah's impatience drove her to get ahead of God and produce Ishmael, who was not the child of promise. Any product or program of our own will, power, and scheming is a work of the flesh.
It is characterized by strife, contention, and jealousy.

The peace of God is missing because God himself is not in it. Therefore, have patience. Wait for God's perfect timing and provision, a work done by the Spirit of God.

Genesis 16

36.

Our homes need to be kept holy before the Lord. If we want to experience His presence, we must rid our homes of any unclean articles: idols, pornography, pagan artifacts, or occult items. Unclean articles invite the presence of demonic activity into our homes. These spirits will try to destroy us. If we choose to co-habit with them, God will not fight for us, nor deliver our enemies into our hands. As in the Garden of Eden before Adam sinned, God wants to live among us, talk to us, and commune with us. He wants us to be holy as He is holy, and our homes must be holy as well for Him to abide with us. His manifest presence is felt when our homes and our lives are clean and undefiled.

Genesis 3; Deuteronomy 23:14; Joshua 8, 23:12-13

37.

The Lord has the power to control our enemies for His purposes. Sometimes He hardens their hearts toward us so we will destroy them. At other times He causes them to live at peace with us. When a man's ways are pleasing to the Lord, even his enemies will have respect for him. Then there are times when the enemy is allowed to harass us and tempt us away from God. This is called a test; one allowed by God to prove what is in our heart.

See Exodus, the story of Pharaoh against the Israelites, and Job, the story of his time of testing.

38.

At different times throughout our life, God tests us to prove what is really in our heart. The test with the daily provision of manna in the wilderness proved whether or not the Israelites would follow His instructions. Job was tested to see if he would curse God for all his misfortune. Abraham was tested for his obedience and whether he feared God more than he loved his son. The test is not so God will know what is in our heart, for He already knows the deep things within us. The test is so we will know for a certainty that we can trust and obey him no matter what the trial.

Exodus 16; Job 1-2, 5:17

39.

God wants to heal us, but we have to take the time to reach out and touch the hem of His garment. We must choose to believe before we can receive. We have to exercise our faith first and believe for healing. If the healing does not come when we expect it to, ask the Holy Spirit if there is any sin or other hindrance that is keeping us from receiving our healing. Perhaps there is something we will need to change first, or some act of obedience that we must comply with, before God will heal us. After all, it is so much easier to put our faith in medicine and doctors than in the direct healing power of Jesus Christ. And it's certainly more convenient to take a pill than to spend the time in prayer seeking God for results.

Matthew 9:21, 21:22; James 5:15

40.

"Stop, drop, and roll." These are the instructions firemen give elementary students when they visit the school to teach them about fire safety. Following this simple rule when our clothes are on fire can save our life. This is a great rule to practice in our spiritual life as well. When we find ourselves in conflict, turmoil, or danger, we should stop what we are doing, drop to our knees in prayer, and roll with whatever the Holy Spirit tells us to do. "To roll with" means to obey, to take action, to comply. The Spirit may tell us to surrender, to repent, to show the fruit of the Spirit, or to do battle with the enemy until righteousness, peace, and joy are once again established.

John 14:26; Romans 14:17

41.

Some nations have a destiny of death, destruction, destitution, and bondage. According to Genesis 9 and 10, certain nations, civilizations, and family lines are under the curse of Canaan. God has ordained it since the days of Noah. However, He also sent His son Jesus Christ to be the sacrificial lamb for our sins so we could be freed from these curses. We serve a god of justice and a god of mercy. We may be born into the iniquity of our forefathers, but if we call upon Jesus Christ we can be born again into the kingdom of God. All those who call upon the name of the Lord shall be saved.

Joel 2:32; John 3: 16

42.

Jesus baptizes us in the Holy Spirit for two purposes. First, it is so we will be filled with power, wisdom, and truth. Secondly, it is so we can bless others with the gifts of the Spirit. These gifts are given not for our own benefit, but for the benefit of others. Jesus taught His disciples to pray the Lord's Prayer and then told them a story about a man who went to his friend's house at midnight to ask for bread. His friend needed three loaves of bread to take on his journey. The neighbor responded to his friend's boldness and concern for another's need. God responds to our requests when we come boldly asking for help to meet the need of others.

The gifts of discernment, prophecy, words of wisdom, or miracles could be just the things someone needs to receive from you. Don't be caught in the middle of the night with nothing to give to someone else in need. Ask Jesus to baptize you in the Holy Ghost so you can have boldness and His gifts to share with others.

Luke 11:13

43.

Have you been established in the kingdom? In Luke 13, Jesus tells us what the kingdom of God is like. He compares it to a mustard seed that a man took and planted in his garden. It grew, became a tree and the birds perched in its branches. That mustard tree provided protection, shade, and a place of rest for God's little creatures. Likewise, if we are established in the kingdom of God, all our needs will be met by a loving and wise Father who knows what we need even before we do.

Matthew 6:33; Romans 14:17

44.

Which group will you be in during the millennium? Jesus told us the parable of the ten minas to illustrate what would happen to three types of people on judgment day when He comes to set up His millennium reign. His faithful servants will be given various numbers of cities over which to rule, depending on their trustworthiness here on earth. The second group is composed of people who were unfaithful and irresponsible with what God gave them. They will not be given any authority or responsibility to rule and reign with Jesus. The third group consists of Jesus' enemies. They will be brought before Him to be destroyed and no longer allowed to remain on earth.

Luke 19:11-27

45.

Fulfilling our destiny will mean laying down our life for others. On September 11, 2001, a small group on a Pan American flight was determined to overcome the terrorists who had taken control of their plane. After assessing the dangerous situation and coming up with a plan, they proclaimed "Let's roll!" History records that they were willing to stand up against and overcome the enemy at all costs to their own lives. They were fighting for a cause they believed in and gave their lives to protect our nation's capital. Scripture commands us to love each other as Christ loved us. "Greater love has no one than this, that he lay down his life for his friends."

John 15:11-13

46.

Faith is a muscle that grows with exercise. When we have a need that we can't provide for ourselves, then we go to Him in prayer. One September morning, I planned on making some homemade peach ice cream to take to a Labor Day picnic at our neighbor's house. At the time, we were living in the woods of rural Georgia. I drove twelve miles to town to buy fresh peaches and was greatly disappointed when there were none at the grocery store.

On the way back home, I prayed. "Lord, I need some peaches. Please, show me where I can find some." His reply was, "Stop at Mrs. Black's house. She can help you." Sure enough, she was home and had a late blooming peach tree in her back yard. Delighted to be of help to me, she gave me a basket full—free for the asking. God's provision is available to us—free for the asking, because He delights in meeting all our needs.

Philippians 4:19,
"My God will meet all your needs according to His glorious riches in Christ Jesus."

47.

Resurrection Day can come any day of the year. For someone to become a believer and experience the resurrection power of Christ, three things have to happen. 1) The Holy Spirit has to open their blind eyes and minds to reveal their need for Jesus Christ as Savior. 2) They have to invite Christ to live in them acknowledging He died for their sins. 3) They have to ask the Holy Spirit to fill them with His enabling power. That's what being "born again" is all about.

John 3:3, 16:7-15; Acts 1:8

48.

To be transformed, our minds have to be renewed by the Word and our spirit has to be empowered by the Holy Spirit. Many Christians live way below their potential in Christ and their inheritance in the kingdom of God. Churches are full of people who come regularly, listen to the sermon, sing the hymns, and even tithe faithfully. Yet, they are bound in tradition, serving God on their own terms, and spiritually blind. Come Holy Spirit and save us from ourselves!

Romans 12:1-2; Acts 1:4-8

49.

Great distress in lives can mean we have forsaken God and are living our life independently of Him. When we bow down and serve other gods, the one true, living God will not stand and fight for us. We are on our own and subject to the evil, demonic forces we are serving. According to the scriptures, God will hand us over to our enemies. Other gods can include the pursuit of education, power, fame, fortune, sexuality, self-interests, or involving ourselves in the occult. God is a god of mercy and of judgment. We can turn away from God or pursue God. He may allow our enemies to pursue us, and we will reap destruction from our own choices. The Solution: a deep, sincere repentance from our sins and crying out to God for His intervention. Acknowledge we have sinned against Him, ask for forgiveness, and plead for His mercy and grace.

Joshua 23:12-13

50.

The kingdom of God must be established in us first before we can be used to establish it in the earth. The kingdom of God is righteousness, peace, and joy in the Holy Ghost. If our lives do not reflect these three attributes, how can we influence others? As ambassadors of His kingdom, we must be walking in the fullness of the Spirit to have a positive effect on the world around us. When Christian parents complain and get discouraged that their children are not following after God like they did, maybe it is because they never truly demonstrated victorious, kingdom living in their own lives. Prayer: "Dear God, let your kingdom be established in me. Let Christ rule and reign in my heart and mind. Let everything I do and say bring you glory and reflect the life of Christ."

Romans 14:17

51.

God knows the end from the beginning and has a divine plan already set in motion. Just before the Israelites crossed the River Jordan to take possession of their promised land, they camped at a place called Shittim. The Lord commanded them to consecrate themselves before going into battle. The word shittim in Hebrew means "to pierce, to scourge, to flog." That is a description of what Jesus experienced when he was crucified on the Cross two thousand years later. He was the sacrificial lamb slain for us so we can be forgiven and cleansed from our sins. As we appropriate His atonement for our sins and consecrate ourselves to His service, God will dwell among us. He will lead us into battle and enable us to overcome all our enemies.

Joshua 3; Exodus 29; Matthew 1:23

52.

Are you experiencing a fulfillment of all the promises of God or just some of them? Is your life characterized by success, financial prosperity, Godly relationships, good health, and holiness? Do you feel blessed above and beyond what you could ever hope for or expect? If not, the reason could be you haven't destroyed all your enemies and taken possession of your inheritance in the kingdom of God. Satan and his spirits have come to kill, steal, and destroy God's people and keep them from experiencing the fullness of the promises. God planned for us to enjoy the abundant life through His son, Jesus Christ. Ask the Holy Spirit to reveal any areas where you have allowed the enemy to rob you, to control your behavior, or keep you in bondage, thereby reaping destruction in your life. God promises to give your enemies into your hands so you can destroy them. Asking God to do something is like asking Him to drive the car for you while you sit there and watch. He has done everything He already needs to do, and it is up to you to appropriate the victory by going to war against your enemy. When you have destroyed your enemies and their influence on you, then you will experience the fullness of the promises.

Deuteronomy 28; Joshua 1:1-11; John 10:10

53.

When a nation's leader sins against God's commandments, both he and the people can suffer punishment. The scriptures give us many examples of God's judgment by famine, floods, plagues, or attack by our enemies. These curses are brought on by disobedience to God's laws. The same is true of the head of a family, a church, or other organization. One example comes to mind from Joshua's life. He made a covenant with the Gibeonites not to kill them, which went strictly against what God had told him to do. They were allowed to live among the Israelites as laborers instead. Years later, Saul in his zeal for Israel, annihilated the Gibeonites, breaking the covenant Joshua had made. In Samuel 21, we read that during David's reign, there was a famine for three successive years. The reason why? It was the result of Saul's disobedience to the Lord. The family of God suffered famine and death because of his failure to obey God. The curse was finally broken when David made restitution to the Gibeonites. Rain once again poured down from heaven, and God answered prayer on behalf of the land.

Deuteronomy 28; Joshua 9; Samuel 21

54.

Water, water everywhere, but are you drinking in? Water is the most precious element on earth, and without it we would die. With soap and water, we wash our bodies, clothes, cars, pets, and houses. Drinking eight glasses of water a day cleanses our bodies on the inside, removing toxic waste that poisons us. As Christians, we are being contaminated daily by the world and often don't do anything to get detoxified spiritually. But with the water of the Word, we can wash our soul and spirit. We are cleansed by the internal washing of water through the Word. We can then be presented to Christ without stain, wrinkle, and blemish, holy and blameless. As our minds are renewed by the Word, we are transformed into the image of Christ. We begin to think and act like Christ. Also, like Christ, we will offer our bodies as living sacrifices, holy and pleasing to God. This is our spiritual act of worship.

Romans 12:1-2; Ephesians 5:2-6

55.

If you give God the first part of your day, then He will bless you the rest of your day! We humans presume to be in control of our lives and naively think we can get along fine without daily asking for the loving protection and provision of our Heavenly Father. We get up, go to work, and come home each day thinking we are doing just fine without spending time communing with our Father God. As long as things are OK, we don't take time to read His Word or pray.
Warning! Pride goes before a fall. Don't make the mistake of neglecting your spiritual life while in pursuit of natural endeavors. If you want God to bless you every day, spend some time in His Presence acknowledging your love and appreciation for His watch and care over your life.

Proverbs 16:18

Conclusion

One beautiful, autumn afternoon in 1991, my daughter Mary and I were heading home after a day at school. As we were passing over a viaduct, we were struck from behind by a drunk, teenage girl driving seventy miles per hour. Our car spun out of control and rammed into the wall sliding backward along the overpass. I could just imagine us going over the side and landing on the highway below during rush hour traffic.

There wasn't time to pray, quote the Word, or even cry out to God. But in that instant of panic and fear, I heard the Holy Spirit say in a near audible voice, "Just relax. You're going to be alright!"

The car stopped safely but was totally wrecked from the rear bumper forward to just behind our seats. We suffered only minor injuries and temporary trauma to our necks. When the car was towed away, we discovered the words, "Jesus Saves" written in brown paint on the wall in the exact spot where we crashed. Amazingly, it matched the paint scraped off our taupe-colored Taurus. Praise God for His divine intervention and protection!

God spared our lives that day because He has a divine plan and purpose for our existence. My prayer for everyone who reads this devotional book is that they also will discover the plan and purpose God has for them as they fulfill their destiny in the kingdom of God. May these pearls of wisdom guide you along the way.

Thank you, Lord, for your faithfulness to me even when I have not remained as close to you as I should.

Thank you for sparing my life so I could live again to serve you and praise your name.

DEVOTIONS FOR OVERCOMERS

Blessed is the man who finds wisdom,
The man who gains understanding,
For she is more profitable than silver
And yields better returns than gold.
She is more precious than rubies;
Nothing you desire can compare with her.
Long life is in her right hand;
In her left hand are riches and honor.
Her ways are pleasant ways,
And all her paths are peace.
She is a tree of life to those who embrace her;
Those who lay hold of her will be blessed.

Proverbs 3:13-18

Food Timeline

I have been interested in food history for years, and after searching the Internet, I was surprised to find so many food items had been around so long. My thinking only equated a product's time of origin with when I first was introduced to the product via the newspaper, television, or radio, or when I actually saw the product in the store. Many products, like our Anne's products, start out as a regional product, then branch into expanded markets. As the product is introduced into new areas, customers think it is a brand new product. We are not a nationally distributed product at this time, and as we are introduced into new markets, we are seen as a new product in that area.

I want to thank Lynne and Robin for allowing me to use their research to put together this food timeline.

In the beginning, there was:

Water	Eggs and insects	Nuts	Spices
Salt	Fruits and vegetables	Sheep, pigs, cows, fowl	Oils
Shellfish and fish	Grains	Milk	

By the first century, cooking was in full swing:

Fried chicken	Rice pudding	Omelets
Italian wedding soup	Cheesecake	

The second century through the fourteenth century brought many new tastes into being:

Sushi	Corned beef	Lasagna	Crumpets
Pretzels	Hamburgers	Pancakes	Gingerbread
Coffee	Kabobs	Waffles	Couscous
Baklava	Ravioli	Apple pie	Applesauce

The fifteenth through seventeenth centuries, as man began to travel more, brought forth even more exotic dishes:

Salsa	Teriyaki chicken	Chess pie	Lemonade
Quiche	Sweet potatoes	Shortbread	Croissants
Puff pastry	Vanilla	French onion soup	Potato salad

1876	Saltine crackers	1920	LaChoy food products	1937	A&P grocery stores
1881	Pillsbury flour	1921	Betty Crocker	1937	Kraft macaroni and cheese
1886	Coca Cola	1921	Eskimo Pie	1937	Pepperidge Farm
1888	Log Cabin syrup	1921	Hershey's Kisses get the	1937	Ragu Spaghetti sauce
1889	McCormick spices		paper streamer	1937	Spam
1890	Knox gelatin	1921	Land O'Lakes butter	1938	Teflon
1891	Del Monte	1921	Sue Bee honey	1938	Nescafé instant coffee
1891	Fig Newtons	1921	White Castle hamburger	1939	Lay's potato chips
1891	Quaker Oats Company		restaurant	1939	Nestle chocolate chips
1895	Shredded coconut	1921	Wrigley's gum	1939	Pressure cooker
1896	Cracker Jack	1924	Bit-O-Honey	1940	Dairy Queen
1896	Tootsie Rolls	1925	Wesson oil	1941	"M & M's" chocolate
1897	Campbell's tomato soup	1926	Hormel canned ham		candies
1897	Jello	1926	Milk Duds	1945	Tupperware
1900	Chiclets gum	1927	Gerber baby food	1947	Aluminum foil
1900	Hershey's chocolate bar	1927	Kool-Aid	1949	Minute rice
1902	Barnum's animal crackers	1927	Lender's bagels	1949	Pillsbury Bake-Off
1902	Karo corn syrup	1928	Butterfinger	1950	Dunkin' Donuts
1902	Pepsi	1928	Reese's peanut butter cups	1952	Kellogg's Frosted Flakes
1904	Dr. Pepper	1928	Rice Krispies	1955	Kentucky Fried Chicken
1904	Popcorn	1928	Velveeta cheese	1958	Jif peanut butter
1906	Kellogg's Corn Flakes	1929	Klondike bar	1963	Chips Ahoy cookies
1907	Hershey's Kisses	1929	Oscar Mayer wieners	1963	Self-cleaning ovens
1908	Dixie paper cups	1930	Bisquick	1965	Cool Whip whipped
1909	Lipton tea	1930	Snickers		topping
1910	Tea bags	1930	Toll House cookies	1970	Hamburger Helper
1911	Crisco	1930	Hostess Twinkies	1971	Starbucks
1912	Hamburger buns	1932	Corn chips	1976	Jelly Belly
1912	Hellmann's mayonnaise	1933	7-Up	1981	Anne's Flat Dumplings
1912	Life Savers	1933	V8 juice	1981	Aspartame
1912	Morton table salt	1933	Waldorf salad	1985	Pop Secret microwave
1913	Oreo cookies	1934	Ritz crackers		popcorn
1915	Processed cheese	1934	Sugar Daddy	1993	The Food Network
1917	Clark bar	1935	Five-flavor Life Savers	1996	Olestra
1917	Moon Pie	1936	Borden's Elsie the cow	1998	WOW potato chips
1919	Sunkist oranges	1936	Girl Scout cookies	2000	Precut celery and carrot
1920	Wonder Bread	1936	Mars bars		sticks

Awards and Recognition

March 31, 1988
The Flavors of Carolina
Commissioner's Award
Most Creative Exhibit

January 24, 1989
The Flavors of Carolina
The NC Department of
Agriculture
Commissioner's Award
Most Creative Exhibit

September 17, 1991
Presented by Ayden Business Leaders
In recognition of excellent leadership in private enterprise and outstanding commitment of business and community service activities in Ayden

September 17, 1991
Presented by Pitt-Greenville
Chamber of Commerce
Pitt County Business leaders
In recognition of excellent leadership in private enterprise and outstanding commitment of business and community service activities in Ayden

1991
Leadership in Entrepreneurial Achievement and Philanthropy Award

May 1992
Article in *Entrepreneurial Magazine*
Article in *Entrepreneurial Woman Magazine*

1992
U.S. Small Business Administration
Small Business Week Award presented to Bryan and Anne Grimes,
Small Business Persons of the Year of North Carolina
In recognition of your contributions to the strengthening of small business

March 21, 1993
Harvey's Supermarkets
Anne's Flat Dumplings awarded the Customer Service Award in the Food category at Harvey's Second Annual Home and Health Show

1993
Entrepreneur of the Year awarded to Mildred Anne Grimes, Harvest Time Foods, Inc.
Honoring those individuals and companies whose ingenuity, hard work, and innovation have created successful and growing business ventures

1994
Anne Grimes inducted into the Goodness Grows in North Carolina Hall of Fame

March 1995
Harvest Time Foods, Inc.
Awarded Business of the Month by the Ayden Chamber of Commerce

May 2, 1996
U.S. Department of Justice
U.S. Attorney's Office
Eastern District of North Carolina
Certificate of Appreciation presented to Harvest Time Foods, Inc., for outstanding contributions to the Greenville Weed and Seed Initiative's Community Clean Up Project

2002
Anne's Dumplings
In appreciation for your sponsorship for the 2002 Ayden Fall Ball

February 2006
Certificate of Appreciation for twenty-five years of contributions to Pitt County presented to Harvest Time Foods, Inc., by the Pitt County Development Commission

Index

Anne's Capsicana Sauce
Barbecue Chicken, 85
Capsicana Dip, 94
Pork Loin, 88

Anne's Chicken Base
Alfredo Sauce with
Dumplings, 89
Anne's Potato Soup, 94
Chicken and Dressing
Casserole, 85
Chicken Fricassee, 83
Chicken 'n Dumplings
Soup, 82
Corn Chowder, 93
E-Z Chicken 'n
Dumplings, 82
Oyster Fritters, 89
Peas 'n Dumplings, 92

Anne's Flat Dumplings
Alfredo Sauce with
Dumplings, 89
Chicken 'n Dumplings
Soup, 82
E-Z Chicken 'n Dumplings, 82
Lasagna, 90
Old-Fashioned Chicken 'n
Dumplings, 81
Pork Backbone 'n
Dumplings, 87
Ravioli, 90
Sausage 'n Dumplings
Casserole, 88

Skillet Beef 'n Dumplings, 86
Spinach 'n Dumplings
Casserole, 92
Steak-umms Casserole, 86

**Anne's Flat Dumpling
Strips**
Baked Pastry Strips, 95
Country Ham 'n
Dumplings, 87
Fried Pastry Strips, 95
Peas 'n Dumplings, 92

Appetizers
Crispy Cheese
Crackers, 100
Veggie Bars, 100

Banana
Banana Nut Bread, 102

Beef
Corned Beef
Hash, 105
Hot Beef Spread, 101
Hot Dog Chili, 106
Skillet Beef 'n
Dumplings, 86
Steak-umms Casserole, 86

Berry
Boiled Berry Cobbler with
Fried Pastry Strips, 97
Strawberry Delight, 97

Beverages
Bedtime Milk Toddy, 11

Breads
Banana Nut Bread, 102
Coffee Cake Muffins, 104
Schoolhouse Rolls, 102

Broccoli
Veggie Bars, 100

Cakes
1-2-3-4 Cake, 124
Anne's Vanilla Wafer Cake, 124
Coconut Pineapple Cake, 126
Grandma Briley's Orange
Cake with Meringue, 127
Mother's Exquisite Coconut
Cake, 125

Candy
Caramels, 117
Confetti Fudge, 119
Divinity, 117
Double Peanut Clusters, 120
Judy's Velveeta Cheese
Fudge, 118
Microwave Peanut
Brittle, 122
Mother's Chocolate Fudge, 27
Peanut Butter Balls, 120
Peanut Butter Fudge, 119
Praline Fudge, 119
Pralines, 121

Cauliflower
Veggie Bars, 100

Cheese
Baked Macaroni and
    Cheese, 111
Crispy Cheese Crackers, 100
Judy's Velveeta Cheese
    Fudge, 118
Peanut Butter Fudge, 119
Veggie Bars, 100

Chicken
Barbecue Chicken, 85
Chicken and Dressing
    Casserole, 85
Chicken Fricassee, 83
Chicken 'n Dumplings
    Soup, 82
E-Z Chicken 'n Dumplings, 82
Old-Fashioned Chicken 'n
    Dumplings, 81

Chocolate
Anne's Chocolate
    Meringue Pie, 129
Becky's Chocolate
    Chess Pie, 128
Double Peanut
    Clusters, 120
Forgotten Cookies, 116
Judy's Velveeta Cheese
    Fudge, 118
Mother's Chocolate Biscuit
    Pudding, 134
Peanut Butter Balls, 120

Coconut
Anne's Vanilla Wafer
    Cake, 124
Coconut Pie, 131
Mother's Exquisite Coconut
    Cake, 125

Collards
Collards, 108

Cookies
Bobby's Nutty Fingers, 112
Brown Sugar Cookies, 114
Drop Butter Wafers, 112
Forgotten Cookies, 116

Cookies, Bar
Becky's Chewy Bar
    Cookies, 115
Carole's Blonde Brownies, 38

Corn
Corn Chowder, 93
Corn Fritters, 108
Mother's Corn Pudding, 109

Desserts. *See also* Cakes;
    Candy; Cookies; Pies
Boiled Berry Cobbler with
    Fried Pastry Strips, 97
Grandma Taylor's
    Old-Fashioned Tea
    Cakes, 18
Mother's Chocolate Biscuit
    Pudding, 134
Pecan Tart, 133

Pootabear's Pineapple
    Stuffing, 134
Strawberry Delight, 97

Dips
Capsicana Dip, 94
Hot Beef Spread, 101
Hot Crab Dip, 101

Fish
Daddy's Fish Stew, 107
Salmon Cakes, 106

Frostings/Icings
Cream Cheese Frosting, 126
Italian Meringue Icing, 125

Fruit. *See also* Banana; Berry;
    Coconut; Orange; Peach;
    Pineapple
Confetti Fudge, 119

Ham
Collards, 108
Country Ham 'n
    Dumplings, 87

Orange
Grandma Briley's
    Orange Cake with
    Meringue, 127
Peggy's Orange Icebox Pie, 130

Peach
Grandma Taylor's Peach
    Pandowdy, 135

Peanut Butter
Double Peanut Clusters, 120
Peanut Butter Balls, 120
Peanut Butter Fudge, 119

Peanuts
Double Peanut Clusters, 120
Microwave Peanut Brittle, 122

Peas
Peas 'n Dumplings, 92

Pecans
Anne's Vanilla Wafer Cake, 124
Banana Nut Bread, 102
Bobby's Nutty Fingers, 112
Brown Sugar Cookies, 114
Forgotten Cookies, 116
Judy's Velveeta Cheese
Fudge, 118
Pecan Pie, 131
Pecan Tart, 133
Praline Fudge, 119
Pralines, 121

Pies
Anne's Chocolate
Meringue Pie, 129
Basic Meringue, 132
Becky's Chocolate
Chess Pie, 128
Chess Pie, 131
Coconut Pie, 131
David's Sweet Potato Pie, 130
Grandma Taylor's Peach
Pandowdy, 135

Pecan Pie, 131
Peggy's Orange Icebox
Pie, 130

Pineapple
Banana Nut Bread, 102
Coconut Pineapple
Cake, 126
Ilene's Watergate Salad, 104
Pootabear's Pineapple
Stuffing, 134

Pork. *See also* Ham; Sausage
Pork Backbone 'n
Dumplings, 87
Pork Loin, 88

Potatoes
Anne's Potato Soup, 94
Corn Chowder, 93
Corned Beef Hash, 105
Daddy's Fish Stew, 107

Salads
Anne's Cucumber-Onion-
Tomato Salad, 105
Ilene's Watergate Salad, 104
Mother's Lettuce Slaw, 22

Sausage
Sausage 'n Dumplings
Casserole, 88

Seafood. *See also* Fish
Hot Crab Dip, 101
Oyster Fritters, 89

Side Dishes
Baked Macaroni and
Cheese, 111

Soups
Anne's Potato Soup, 94
Chicken 'n Dumplings
Soup, 82
Corn Chowder, 93
Daddy's Fish Stew, 107

Spinach
Spinach 'n Dumplings
Casserole, 92

Sweet Potatoes
David's Sweet Potato Pie, 130
Sweet Potato Soufflé, 109

Tomatoes
Anne's Cucumber-Onion-
Tomato Salad, 105
Stewed Tomatoes, 110
Veggie Bars, 100

Vegetables. *See* Broccoli;
Cauliflower; Collards;
Corn; Peas; Potatoes;
Spinach; Sweet Potatoes;
Tomatoes

To order additional copies of

and to order our products, please visit our Web site at
www.annesdumplings.com.
Payment may be made through PayPal.